Something to Remember You By

A Play

Jimmie Chinn

A Samuel French Acting Edition

SAMUELFRENCH-LONDON.CO.UK
SAMUELFRENCH.COM

Copyright © 1996 by Jimmie Chinn
All Rights Reserved

SOMETHING TO REMEMBER YOU BY is fully protected under the copyright laws of the British Commonwealth, including Canada, the United States of America, and all other countries of the Copyright Union. All rights, including professional and amateur stage productions, recitation, lecturing, public reading, motion picture, radio broadcasting, television and the rights of translation into foreign languages are strictly reserved.

ISBN 978-0-573-01872-5

www.samuelfrench-london.co.uk

www.samuelfrench.com

FOR AMATEUR PRODUCTION ENQUIRIES

UNITED KINGDOM AND WORLD EXCLUDING NORTH AMERICA

plays@SamuelFrench-London.co.uk

020 7255 4302/01

Each title is subject to availability from Samuel French,
depending upon country of performance.

CAUTION: Professional and amateur producers are hereby warned that SOMETHING TO REMEMBER YOU BY is subject to a licensing fee. Publication of this play does not imply availability for performance. Both amateurs and professionals considering a production are strongly advised to apply to the appropriate agent before starting rehearsals, advertising, or booking a theatre. A licensing fee must be paid whether the title is presented for charity or gain and whether or not admission is charged.

The professional rights in this play are controlled by Samuel French Ltd, 52 Fitzroy Street, London, W1T 5JR.

No one shall make any changes in this title for the purpose of production. No part of this book may be reproduced, stored in a retrieval system, or transmitted in any form, by any means, now known or yet to be invented, including mechanical, electronic, photocopying, recording, videotaping, or otherwise, without the prior written permission of the publisher. No one shall upload this title, or part of this title, to any social media websites.

The right of Jimmie Chinn to be identified as author of this work has been asserted by him in accordance with Section 77 of the Copyright, Designs and Patents Act 1988

Something To Remember You By

First presented (under another title) by Theatre West Four at The Duke's Head Theatre, Richmond, Surrey, on 18th April 1994, with the following cast:

Armstrong	Mick Cawson
Pearl	Joanne Burnett
Beryl	Pat Nicholls
Venetia	Elicia Daly
O'Toole	Dave Lillie

Directed by Frances Smith
Lighting and Sound by Ricky Gauld

The present, re-written, version was first presented at The Questors Theatre, Ealing, London, on 22nd July 1995, with the following cast:

Armstrong	James Brennan
Pearl	Linda Shannon
Beryl	Sophie James
Venetia	Sara Pruce
O'Toole	Mark Fitzgerald

Directed by Tony Hill
Designed by Spencer Butler
Lighting by Martin Stoner
Sound by Ian Howlett

CHARACTERS

Armstrong Armstrong
Pearl Armstrong
Beryl Armstrong
Venetia Armstrong
O'Toole

The play happens in time and space—sometimes here and now—sometimes there and then

CHARACTER DESCRIPTIONS

Armstrong describes himself on page 2.

Pearl - Armstrong's mother. An ordinary woman—plain with straight dull hair held in place with plastic hair-slides: she wears a wrap-around floral overall over her Sunday best frock which is seen later in the play; on her feet, pink ankle socks and bedroom slippers with pom-poms.

Beryl - Armstrong's sister. Looks like her brother, but older: plain, with glasses, and, like her mother, her hair is held in place with a hair slide; she walks with a slight limp. Her frock is simple until later when she wears a grey two-piece suit with pearls and sensible shoes. She is down-trodden and long-suffering.

Venetia - Armstrong's wife. Very different from the others: brassy, dressed in a tight blouse or jumper displaying breasts which appear to belong to someone else; always wears bright colours and a blonde wig and lip-gloss. She might, from a distance, be mistaken for "Gina Gale" at the height of her fame in the Sixties. In Act II she takes on the appearance of both Pearl and Beryl.

O'Toole A mysterious, almost unknown man in a dark suit who can become anything Armstrong wants him to be. All the characters he plays must speak with an Irish accent.

"GINA GALE"

"Gina Gale" is a fictitious singer, at the height of her fame in the Sixties. Her voice should be full, powerful and wonderfully thrilling - typical of the big-band singers of that period. Pre-recorded songs by a not-easily-identified singer *could* be used, provided a return is made to Phonographic Performance Ltd, but you may well have a good singer available to perform such "torch songs" for you - making a return to the Performing Right Society.

Ideally, the photographs on the record sleeves used in the play should be of the actress playing Venetia in her Act I guise as "Gina Gale".

The songs used should be typical of numbers written in the Thirties and Forties, such as *Something To Remember You By, Someone To Watch Over Me, I'll Get By, Who's Sorry Now* etc.

J.C.

A licence issued by Samuel French Ltd to perform this play does not include permission to use any Incidental music specified in this copy. Where the place of performance is already licensed by the PERFORMING RIGHT SOCIETY a return of the music used must be made to them. If the place of performance is not so licensed, then application should be made to the Performing Right Society, 29 Berners Street, London W1.

A separate and additional licence from PHONOGRAPHIC PERFORMANCE LTD, Ganton House, Ganton Street, London W1 is needed whenever commercial recordings are used.

Other plays by Jimmie Chinn published by
Samuel French Ltd:

After September
Albert Make Us Laugh
But Yesterday
From Here To The Library
Home Before Dark, *or*, **The Saga of Miss Edie Hill**
In By The Half
In Room Five Hundred and Four
Interior Designs
Pity About Kitty
A Respectable Funeral
Straight and Narrow
Take Away The Lady
Too Long An Autumn

To Frances, Joanna, Pat, Elicia, Mick and Dave . . .
for whom it was written.

And to Tony Hill who inspired me
to take a second look.

ACT I

In the darkness we hear the singing voice of "Gina Gale"

The set: at the start of the play, the stage is a simple black void with a table, a chair, a bench and a high stool—all painted black. A black typewriter sits on the table along with a pile of white manuscript

A shaft of Light comes up slowly on the table and chair where Armstrong is pounding away at his typewriter. Standing directly behind him, smoking and impassive, is O'Toole—the smoke from his cigarette curls and rises to meet the lights from above. After a moment, Armstrong becomes aware that he is being watched—he stops typing, sighs with impatience, then starts work again. The music fades away. Silence now except for the pounding of the typewriter

Armstrong (*stopping work*) I know you're watching me and I do wish you wouldn't. You know how I hate being watched!
O'Toole (*with an Irish accent*) Is it finished?
Armstrong How the hell would I know!
O'Toole Nearly finished, perhaps?
Armstrong I don't know, for God's sake! If only you'd just leave me alone...
O'Toole I'm sorry. I'll be quiet. (*He takes a drag on his cigarette and turns slightly up stage*)

Armstrong resumes his typing for a moment, but has obviously lost his flow—he rips the paper from the machine, screws it up and throws it away, picks up the pile of finished manuscript from the table, rises, and moves DR *where a second pool of Light comes up on a high stool. He sits, his knees almost up to his chest and clutches the manuscript close to his body. Silence*

When can I read it?

Armstrong Who said you could? I might not want anyone to read it. It's private.

O'Toole doesn't answer—he wanders L as a third shaft of Light comes up on the bench

I might read you a bit of it ... but only a bit and only when I feel like it.

O'Toole sits on the bench in silence

I see. Gone all moody have we? The silent treatment again, is it?

O'Toole, stubbing out his cigarette, tries to appear uninterested

OK, then. I'll read you the first page—but that's all you're getting—right? (*From a pocket he produces a pair of old-fashioned wire glasses, puts them on, and holds up his manuscript, ready to read from it*) Ready...?

No answer

Well...?
O'Toole I'm ready.
Armstrong (*coughing politely, then beginning*) "His name was Armstrong. In fact, both his names were Armstrong. Armstrong Armstrong." (*He looks over at O'Toole as if for approval*) "At school, this had worried him slightly—but now he was grown up he felt it had a certain ring to it—an air of quiet sophistication—it made him feel special—placed him in the upper bracket—above the commonplace—superior to those unfortunate enough to be saddled with two or three different names..." (*To O'Toole*) Are you listening or what?

O'Toole looks across at him, but says nothing

"Armstrong had always been small—small and thin—weedy almost—with a lack-lustre personality, little or no confidence and always painfully shy in front of strangers."

We soon realise all this is a clear description of himself

Act I

"His hair always lay flat and shiny on his head and he wore a pair of old-fashioned wire glasses, unflattering corduroy trousers and an unironed shirt with a frayed collar. Until the age of fifteen he hadn't even worn underpants. His mother had considered them an unnecessary extravagance. Perhaps the oddest thing about Armstrong was his face——"

O'Toole Is this you…?

Armstrong (*annoyed*) Sorry…?

O'Toole You. Are you writing about yourself?

Armstrong No. Why should it be me? I'm a writer. I invent. I make things up. That's what writers do. Prick!

O'Toole turns away slightly, maybe lights another cigarette

You hate me, don't you? You really hate me. And don't deny it because it's obvious. Well, bollocks! (*He holds the manuscript close to his chest again, intending to read no further*)

O'Toole No, please. I like it. It sounds good.

Armstrong (*a sucker for praise*) Do you think so—really?

O'Toole I do. Your best so far. What about the other characters—who are they?

Armstrong All in good time—give us a chance. (*He begins to read again, but it is now obvious that he knows his script off by heart*) "Armstrong had always worn glasses—that had been the trouble. Without glasses he felt he could have made it—become a force in the land maybe. A politician perhaps—a magistrate—a newspaper tycoon—or, with a bit of luck, a murderer. Anything, in fact, other than what he was—a nothing—a nobody. He might even have considered being a film star, but he left all that sort of nonsense to Venetia…"

The Light around him grows brighter, warmer now

Venetia, dressed in her "Gina Gale" gear, enters and sits on the corner of his table, chewing gum and doing her nails

"Venetia had always wanted to become a film star. She even dressed like one—walked like one—talked like one…"

Venetia gives the audience a wink, a wiggle and a huge film star smile, then continues to do her nails

"No, Armstrong had made up his mind—it was definitely the glasses that had held him back. He'd worn them since he was——"

Pearl hurries on, carrying a carpet sweeper and a duster etc. and joins Armstrong in his light, speaking as she enters

Pearl Nine. He's worn glasses since he was nine. "This child's bosseyed", the school nurse said to me, "we must put him in glasses at once!"

Armstrong, from here on, becomes the character, abandons the script and speaks from memory

Armstrong It made it difficult when we had Games. Not that I liked Games very much—but it did make it difficult. Having to remove my glasses in case a stray cricket ball caught me in the face.
Venetia (*to the audience*) Don't ever mention his face, whatever you do!
Armstrong No—football, cricket, tennis, golf—you name it—anything to do with balls and I was completely unimpressed.
O'Toole This *is* you, then...?

The other three all round on him and glare furiously

Armstrong
Pearl } (*together*) Just shut it!
Venetia

O'Toole holds up a hand by way of apology

Pearl (*to the audience*) Well, of course, he reads a lot. He's always read a lot has Armstrong. At the age of two I left him in the other room playing with his Meccano and when I got back he was flicking through his dad's book on Dr Crippen ... ever so nonchalant.

Armstrong smiles angelically

Armstrong They sent me to cookery in the end—Mr Palethorpe thought I might like it better. "More up your street, Armstrong," he said. But I couldn't get on with it—my scones didn't rise and my Apricot Surprise was a disaster—and when I spilt melted margarine all over Mrs Clitterhouse she chucked me out!

Act I 5

Pearl What a cow she was. I never liked her.

Beryl hurries on, slightly flustered by being late on cue, and joins Pearl beside Armstrong

Beryl (*to the audience*) "My brother's a special case," I said to Mr Lumsworthy——
Pearl (sotto *to Beryl*) You're late!
Beryl (*trying not to hear this*) "He's been fragile and delicate from birth," I told him. He was a 'special needs' case long before they knew what a 'special needs' was. (*She attempts a weak smile*) I'm Beryl Armstrong... Armstrong's older sister...
Pearl These people have paid good money, Beryl—they're not interested in you!
Armstrong (*ignoring this*) No, well, I was always quite shy, you see. Not altogether backward—backward is something else—but low-key I suppose you'd call it—behind-the-door perhaps—insignificant. I know what had caused it—they knew at school what had caused it. It was my dad ... he'd left us, you see...
Pearl The bastard!
Armstrong Left us in the lurch when I was about five and our Beryl was...
Pearl Ten. Armstrong was five and our Beryl was ten. And there was me without a crust to put in those poor kiddies' mouths.

During the following, Pearl produces a crumpled note from her pinny pocket

Armstrong He was fed up, you see ... left a note saying he was fed up ... a note ... on the mantelpiece—by the clock—and all it said was...
Pearl (*reading the note*) "Fed up ... life's a disappointment—hopped it—am starting a new life in Bangkok with O'Toole!"

O'Toole turns and looks over at Armstrong

Armstrong Mum was devastated...
Pearl What a bugger, eh?
Armstrong Mortified...
Pearl Isn't he a bugger...?
Armstrong And very upset...

Pearl Bangkok—I'll Bangkok him!
Armstrong Suddenly—just like that—and through no fault of her own—there she was—alone in the world and landed with me and our Beryl.
Beryl She'd become a one-parent family long before they knew what a one-parent family looked like.

Pearl, holding a hanky to her mouth, takes a loud sharp intake of breath to stifle her tears

Armstrong Life was different after Dad left—not that I can remember what it was like before he left, but Mum was forever saying...
Pearl (*through her tears*) "Life's not the same since that selfish swine left!"
Armstrong And, of course, because we didn't have much money coming in, she had to find a little part-time job. She knew a woman called Norah Skate who worked part-time peeling onions for the Pixie Pickle factory on Albatross Street...
Pearl "You'll smell to high heaven, Pearl", she said, "you'll smell and you'll cry your friggin' eyes out, but the money's good and you won't even have to leave home," she said. "They deliver the onions straight to your door—you peel 'em and they're back next morning to collect..."
Armstrong Well, it was ideal...
Beryl The perfect solution...
Venetia (*still doing her nails*) Talk about the pits—I wouldn't have done it!
Pearl (*a cry to heaven*) "Everything will be nonchalant from now on..."
Armstrong "She cried." For years our house smelt of onions—and to this day the very sight of a pickle turns my stomach, but we did what we could to help ... me and our Beryl.
Beryl I'd come home from school—cook the tea—do my homework at the table—then lend Mum a helping hand with the onions.
Pearl She was useless...
Armstrong And I did all I could, but the smell knocked you back...
Pearl That lad was a godsend—a treasure—a paragon—he was. He'd sit for hours on end peeling away with me—tears running down his little face...
Venetia Don't mention his face!
Pearl (*lowering her voice*) He was a little jewel—he was—a little star.
Armstrong So ... you see—that's how life was for us: simple—ordinary—deprived.

Act I 7

Pearl Mind you—we never went short—there was always food on that table—a fire in the hearth—a stocking at Christmas.
Beryl An apple—an orange—and some nuts.
Pearl (*to Beryl; furiously*) It's all I could manage—you ungrateful bitch!
Armstrong But at least we always had one thing to look forward to—one night of magic—one evening's escape from the dreary routine of peeling onions, bed and school—school and bed...
Venetia We never got much of *that*, I can tell you!

Pearl glares at her

Armstrong Once a week—usually on a Tuesday—we went to the pictures—the Essoldo on Bass Street. Our night in Paradise I used to call it. A seat in the stalls—a Mars bar and some Butterkist—an ice-lolly in the break—just in time for the big picture—what more could anybody want? And we always sat alone—the three of us...
Venetia Because of the pong I suppose...
Beryl We liked James Bond best—007 ... he was ever so handsome...
Armstrong I liked the girls ... lying stretched out on beds wearing only their nighties with ever such massive looly-bongers!
Pearl (*hitting him*) Armstrong! (*Then to the audience with a smirk*) He's a devil—he is!
Armstrong I'd have gone every night if I could, but Mum never had the money. I loved it when the lights went down and the curtains parted—and when that lion roared or that chap dressed only in his swimming trunks struck that big brass gong. And the glow of the usherettes' torches as they showed people to their seats...
Pearl He wrote this himself, you know.
Armstrong But most of all I liked it in there because I felt safe—no-one was staring at me.

Pearl and Beryl dread what's coming next

Sitting there—in the Essoldo—warm and cosy—no-one was bothered that I was different—no-one was even aware of my dreadful affliction...
Venetia (*rolling her eyes to heaven*) Here we go. Him and his sodding affliction!
Armstrong (*becoming worked up*) I know I was born with it—so it can't

be helped—but however hard I tried I just couldn't put it to the back of my mind. The other kids laughed at me—threw empty tin cans at me...
Pearl Swines...!
Armstrong I know I blame it on my glasses—but it's not my glasses—some people can look nice in glasses—sexy even. Me? I've about as much sex appeal as a pile-up on the M1! (*Angry now*) And one day ... one day ... when I meet my Maker ... when I confront Him face to face... I shall put it to Him... "Why did you do this to me?", I shall say. "Why me? Why not our Beryl? Why did you choose me to be afflicted thus? This is what you did to me—this is the burden I've had to carry through life—this is why I've been such a failure!"

The Light on the group turns blood red as Armstrong turns the upstage side of his face to show the audience—pulling at the skin to distort it. A dramatic chord of music sounds—Phantom-of-the-Opera-ish. *Pearl, Beryl and Venetia recoil in mock horror, hands up to shield them from the "awful" sight*

Pearl (*crying out, "heartbreak" in her voice*) "Armstrong, don't! Don't torture yourself like this...!"

The actors freeze. In the glow of the red light, the sound of Amen Corner singing If Paradise Were Half as Nice *fills the auditorium. Full Lighting slowly comes up as each actor helps to bring Armstrong's living-room-cum-dinette to life. A book-flat, hardly noticeable until now, is opened up to reveal a wall with floral wallpaper and three flying ducks. O'Toole can strike all the black furniture, the typewriter, and lay a small carpet which will define the acting area*

O'Toole exits

An armchair, a small dining table and three chairs, a standard lamp (practical) are all set in place. Beryl spreads a check cloth on the table and sets three places with knives and forks etc. Venetia might use the carpet sweeper here and there. Pearl sets up an ironing board with iron and produces a basket with a pile of clothes etc. All this must be very theatrical and carefully choreographed, using the music—the actors dance as they work and join in the song on cue—the music stops and the cast (except O'Toole who has left the stage) stand frozen in their positions ready to

Act I

continue with the play: Pearl, iron at the ready; Venetia, sitting on the arm of the chair, nail-file poised; Beryl, about to lay two plates of stew on the table; and Armstrong, schoolboy's cap on his head now, is DR *in his own Light ready to address the audience again. The three women remain frozen until given the cue by Armstrong*

Armstrong (*to the audience*) This was our living-room-cum-dinette. We did have another room—a "best" room, but that was saved for when we had visitors. But, because we never had any visitors it was never used at all.

Beryl (*calling, but not moving*) Tea's ready.

Armstrong Life here at Number Thirteen was always the same—dead boring. The routine never varied—me home from school at four—our Beryl home from work at six on the dot. She'd left school at fifteen with two O-levels and a jar of frog-spawn and got a job in the Public Library on Gas Street.

Beryl (*to the audience, thrilled to get her chance to speak, still holding the two plates of stew*) My position was humble at first—making coffee in the mornings with a digestive—tea in the afternoons with a royal tartan shortbread—and as a special treat, I'd make hot, buttered toast if the days were cold and uninviting. Mr Gunter loved my hot, buttered toast. He was the chief librarian—and ever so nice. (*She blushes*)

Pearl (*to Armstrong*) Has she finished or what? Nobody wants to hear all this...

Armstrong (*loudly, clicking his fingers*) Action!

Pearl starts ironing

Beryl places the two plates on the table and exits to the kitchen

Venetia starts doing her nails again, chewing gum as usual. Armstrong goes and sits at the table, knife and fork poised, ready to eat

Pearl (*acting now*) What a life this is... I never flaming well stop. Mrs Jessup has a woman in. She's got a tumble-dryer, a steam iron and an electric toothbrush for God's sake—and what've I got? Sod all. Poverty Hall is this. (*She obviously forgets her lines; to Armstrong*) What's next...?

Venetia "I'm stuck here..."

Pearl I'm stuck here ... all day...
Venetia "Peeling onions—scrimping and scraping"...
Pearl Peeling onions—scrimping and scraping...
Venetia "Manless and celery..."
Pearl Manless and what...?
Venetia Manless and celery, isn't it...?
Armstrong Manless and celibate, you prat!
Venetia Well, at least I know it.
Pearl (*pointing a finger*) Hey, I'm warning you! And anyway—you shouldn't be saying anything—you haven't even arrived yet!
Venetia Well, just imagine I'm not here...

Armstrong and Pearl glare at her

All right—all right—I'm going. (*As she goes, to the audience*) I'll be back later.

Venetia walks off the set as Beryl enters from the kitchen with another plate of stew and sits at the table

Armstrong (*moodily*) What's this mess? I can't eat this.
Beryl (*eating her own*) It's suet dumpling stew with diced carrots. I thought you said you liked it.
Armstrong I expect I did, but I didn't mean I wanted it for ever more. Have you seen this, Mum? Stew again.
Pearl (*coming to the table*) Our Beryl does her best—poor cow. There's cheese and pickles if you don't like it.
Armstrong (*sulking*) No, thanks—I'd rather force this down.
Pearl (*grabbing his cap*) And how many times must I tell you—don't sit at the tea table with your cap on, Armstrong!
Armstrong (*in temper, holding up his knife to her*) I'm going to kill you!

Pearl lands out as if to hit him, but he ducks. All three start to eat in silence

Beryl I'm sorry the gravy's a bit petrified, but I've had one of my sick headaches all day. Mr Gunter wanted to send me home.

Pause as they eat

Did I tell you I've been promoted? Mr Gunter's put me in charge of all the dirty books.

Act I   11

The other two look at her

The soiled books I mean. It'll be my job to take all the books that have become dog-eared and shelf-weary and put them on one side to be given to hospitals or the homeless. Mr Gunter says it's a really responsible job. He says it'll make me a very important pillow of the community.

Armstrong gives the audience a look

Pearl They buried Jessie Cosgrove today.
Beryl Oh, I am sorry. What was the matter with her?
Pearl She was dead. She's never been right since they took her leg off. First it went septic—then gangrenous—then how's-your-father. This is very tasty, our Beryl.
Armstrong (*turning in his chair to address the audience*) This is how it was. Night after night. Forcing down dreadful concoctions rustled up by our Beryl. Endless conversations about people we didn't know who'd either died, got maimed in some terrible accident—or had lost several babies. And everything seemed to happen to somebody else—nothing at all ever happened to us.
Pearl Did I tell you Joyce Cummings has had another miscarriage? They rushed her in, but it was too late.
Beryl She seems really blighted, doesn't she?
Pearl Apparently it's sent him a bit funny. He was caught urinating outside Boots—they had to send for somebody.
Armstrong (*to the audience*) See what I mean...?
Pearl I thought I'd run you up a nice little two-piece, Beryl. To wear at the library. You could look ever so smart. I'll lend you my artificial pearls to go with it. The ones *he* gave me.

The Lights on the living-room fade slightly as Armstrong's Light DR *comes up again*

Armstrong (*rising and walking into his light*) Dad was only ever referred to as "he" ... when *he* was here ... before *he* left us high and dry ... stuff like that. The funny thing is—well, perhaps it isn't funny at all—they never really liked each other anyway. In fact, at times, I used to think she was glad he'd gone. She just couldn't forgive him for leaving us with nothing. But—I mean—what had he...?
Pearl (*calling across time and distance*) A pile of dirty magazines and a box full of old records—that's all your dad left us, Armstrong...

During Armstrong's next speech, Beryl rises, collects the plates etc. and limps off to the kitchen

Pearl goes back to her ironing

Armstrong Mind you—we did have some quite nice times there in the living room at Number Thirteen. Often—in the evenings—after our Beryl had gone to bed—Mum and me used to talk. She'd be peeling onions or making Beryl a new frock for work ... or ironing.

Lights in the living-room come up again, including now the standard lamp which gives the room a cosy evening glow—there is also a glow from the "fire" in the fourth wall

I'd sit on the stool in front of the fire with me legs burning. (*Rolling up his trouser legs, he moves into the scene again and sits in front of the glow from the "fire"*)

His Light fades DR

Mum used to say...
Pearl You'll get corned beef legs in front of that fire...
Armstrong But I never knew what corned beef legs were.

Silence. He gazes into the "fire", while Pearl irons, humming to herself quietly

Mum...?
Pearl Yes, Armstrong.
Armstrong Why did you call me Armstrong?
Pearl Because it's our name.
Armstrong No, you know what I mean. Armstrong Armstrong's a bit of a mouthful, isn't it?
Pearl That was *him*. He was always a bit fanciful—always ... well, a bit of a dreamer. I wanted to call you Trevor, but *he* thought it was too common.
Armstrong (*far away*) I see.
Pearl (*a touchy subject*) You'll soon be leaving school, Armstrong.
Armstrong Thank God.
Pearl Oh now—it can't be that bad.

Act I

Armstrong You must be joking. It's awful. They hate me. They do. Everybody hates me.
Pearl Not everybody, surely. You must have one friend at least.
Armstrong I haven't. Mrs Dooly says I'm a bad influence. She says I'm displaying all the signs of becoming an outcast—a murderer even. She makes the sign of the cross whenever she sees me.
Pearl Now don't exaggerate.
Armstrong I'm not. She hates me.
Pearl Take no notice. It's probably because you're no good at geography.
Armstrong She doesn't teach geography—she teaches religiousness.
Pearl Well, religiousness, then—it's all the same—you're no good at that either.
Armstrong I'm good at English composition. I could be top of the class in that, but Mr Tweedale hates my stories. He says I've got far too vivid an imagination. (*Beat*) Perhaps I could become a writer, eh?
Pearl Now, we don't want any of *that*, Armstrong! Right?
Armstrong But I'd like to be famous for something, Mum. What's the point of being a nobody?
Pearl I'm a nobody. So's our Beryl. There's nothing wrong with being a nobody, Armstrong.
Armstrong Perhaps Mrs Dooly's right—I might put a knife in you and our Beryl and then I'll go down in history. A front page spread in *The Gazette*: "Scar-faced Phantom Slays Mother and Sister—Thousands Flee!"
Pearl You'll have to think about your future sooner or later—you can't keep putting it off.
Armstrong I'm not going to work if that's what you mean. I shall stop at home and become a hermit. Or is that a recluse…?
Pearl Now pack it in, Armstrong! You've got to earn your living somehow. I won't always be here to fend for you.
Armstrong Who'll give me a job? With a face like mine.
Pearl Oh, here we go…
Armstrong I could work somewhere where it's dark, I suppose. Down a coal mine.

Pearl looks to heaven

Or the pictures. I could become an usherette at The Essoldo. Watch the same film fifty times a week!
Pearl You spend too much time in the pictures as it is. Your dad was like

that and look how he ended up—warped in the head. Couldn't you just forget about your face—pretend it isn't there?

Armstrong Forget about it! How can I? You don't know what it's like to be scarred like this. (*He covers the side of his face with his hand*)

Pearl Plenty of people are scarred in some way, Armstrong.

Armstrong Yes, but not in the face.

Pearl Perhaps not. But some people are scarred in other ways. Look at me—you may not be able to see them, but beneath this ironing exterior I carry the scars of life, don't I?

Armstrong (*fascinated by this*) Do you...?

Pearl (*still ironing etc.*) Oh yes. But I soldier on, don't I? Always smiling.

Armstrong Have you never been happy either?

Pearl (*scoffing*) Happy! What's that? Happy's what they are on the pictures, Armstrong. Mind you—I'm quite content I suppose. I'm content now—here with you—I'm content when I go to bingo with Gladys—I'm content at night when I lock that door and put the light out knowing I've got through another day.

Armstrong (*staring into the "fire"*) I know what you mean. Life's a bitch really.

Pearl Oh, come on—you're only young yet—you've got all your future in front of you. You'll see—you'll get a good job—you'll get married—have lovely kiddies.

Armstrong I can't see it, somehow.

Pearl Rubbish. The world's your oyster, Armstrong. Who knows—Miss Right might be waiting to meet you at this very moment...

Armstrong Where though—where?

Pearl What about that nice girl you met at the dance hall—now you liked her.

Ballroom music creeps in as the living-room Lights dip slightly and a brighter pool of Light comes up C

Venetia, dressed for dancing, walks into the pool of light, moving romantically to the music

A mirror ball begins to revolve, catching the coloured lights and adding a touch of ballroom magic

What was her name...?

Act I

Armstrong (*watching Venetia, caught up in the memory*) I don't know... I never spoke to her.
Pearl Didn't you dance with her...?
Armstrong How could I? I'd only sneaked in to watch. Anyway— (*hatred in his voice*)—he was there, wasn't he...?

Venetia dances down stage into an area which is now lit by coloured Lights. Armstrong watches her every move—his eyes aglow with wonder

The music grows louder now as O'Toole, dressed for dancing, enters and joins Venetia on the dance floor. They dance cheek to cheek for a moment

O'Toole (*his Irish accent soft and seductive*) Wouldn't you listen to that music, Venetia? Isn't it grand music? You can't beat the old-fashioned tunes. (*He hums along to the music as his hands start to wander about her body*) Now, wouldn't that music just send you...?
Venetia (*nervous, unsure*) Send me where...?
O'Toole (*hands on her bottom now*) Wouldn't it lift you up to the heavens—right up to the very stars...
Venetia (*shifting his hands*) Here—watch where you're putting yourself.
O'Toole Do you come here often, Venetia? I can't say I've clapped eyes on you before, have I?
Venetia No—it's my very first time—but I am eighteen. Some people don't believe I'm eighteen—they think I'm having them on.
O'Toole Well, I think you're eighteen ... at least I hope you're eighteen. (*Groping her*) You certainly *feel* eighteen—and you're sure *big* enough to be eighteen...

Armstrong looks on—fascinated, but angry

Venetia Here—we'd better be careful—people are watching...
O'Toole Ah, bollocks to 'em—now how about coming outside with me—eh...?
Venetia (*panic in her face*) What for...?
O'Toole You know what for. (*He attempts to put his hand up her skirt*)
Armstrong (*standing up, distressed, calling across time and distance*) Leave her ... you Irish twat—leave her...
Venetia (*kneeing O'Toole in the groin*) Here—stop that, you prick!

O'Toole (*doubled up in agony*) You stupid little bitch—why had you to go an' do that?

Armstrong's Light comes up DR *as he runs across to it*

Armstrong (*calling, delighted*) That's it—that's it. Kick him in the balls!
Venetia (*alone, upset, crying*) Did you see him—did you see what he tried to do? And I'm only fifteen...!

The music suddenly cuts out. Venetia rushes off in tears. O'Toole exits in pain

Black-out except for Armstrong's Light DR *where he stands looking out as if seeing the ballroom in the distance*

Armstrong (*to the audience, alone in his light*) I left school knowing very little about anything and nothing at all about sex. That episode in the Stardust Ballroom was the nearest I'd come to a sexual encounter—apart from Malcolm Bamford at school that is. He'd once asked if he could measure my knodger and when I refused he asked me to measure his. I told him to piss off. At least, even then, I knew I preferred girls to boys and whenever Mr Crompton, our newsagent, wasn't looking I'd nick one of his dirty magazines from the top shelf. They had pictures of women—women with massive looly-bongers—doing this (*he poses seductively*) or this. They all had names like Gloria or Yvette or Lorinda ... never Muriel or Gladys or Ethel like most of the women in our street.

The Lights return to the living-room where Beryl is knitting and Pearl has the local gazette spread out on the ironing board

I was aware though that Mum and our Beryl knew about sex because Mum would often read bits out from the local paper—smutty bits!

Armstrong's Light fades as he enters the scene again and sits on the low stool in front of the "fire". Pearl has her glasses on

Pearl (*reading aloud*) "When charged, the accused had asked for one hundred and twenty three other offences to be taken into consideration. Sentencing him, the magistrate said, 'Not only are you a vile person and

Act I

a pervert of the first water—you are also a menace to society at large. I am sending you to prison for three months and good riddance!'"

Beryl Oh, I say.

Pearl I hope you're not listening to all this, Armstrong. Here's another, Beryl. "Indecent in Shoe Shop" it says… "Bending down to try on a pair of shoes at Freeman, Hardy and Willis's High Street branch last week, customer Mrs Dorothy Leadbetter—pictured above—received the shock of her life. She was indecently exposed to by a man who then fled. Deeply shocked and pale, Mrs Leadbetter—fifty—told our reporter, "He seemed such a nice man at first. He said, 'That's a nice pair you've got there', and of course I thought he was referring to the shoes—but then—and with no prior warning—he dropped his trousers and flashed at me!' Manager of the shop, Mr Arnold Seymore—thirty-five—said 'This kind of thing has got to stop—riff-raff like that should be put away!' Mrs Leadbetter is said to be under sedation at her home in Arlington Drive, Mossley. Police would like to question a man in his early thirties, five feet ten inches tall, who speaks with an Irish accent."

Beryl You're not safe anywhere these days.

Pearl I hope you don't speak to strange men, Armstrong.

Armstrong (*standing on his head or similar*) When do I meet strange men? I never go anywhere.

Pearl No, well—it's a wicked world out there. You're safer indoors.

Beryl Muriel Tate was assaulted in broad daylight in the library. In the passageway between Biographies and Bodily Hygiene. I was on my tea-break at the time, otherwise it might have been me. He was Irish too, I believe.

The Lights fade on the living-room

Pearl and Beryl leave the stage as Armstrong's Light comes up DR

Armstrong (*walking across to his light*) It seems odd now, but looking back on my teenage years I realize that I learned more about life from the pages of *The Gazette* than I did from life itself. At least it taught me two important lessons—never to drop my trousers in public and never to trust men who spoke with an Irish accent. In fact, the less I had to do with the Irish the better. Ironically, and little did I realize it then, but it was one of their number who was eventually going to invade our privacy.

It's Magic *begins to play softly, distant*

It's a night I shall always remember—a night something special happened—something that would change my life forever.

He listens for a moment as the music grows louder

It was about a week before my twentieth birthday, I'd been up in our attic all day—having a scout round—trying to sort out all the junk up there. I was about to give it up as a bad job when ... underneath a pile of old and dusty carpet... I found it. The basket!

The music reaches its height as O'Toole pushes on an old theatrical props basket on castors

Coloured Lights come up on the basket as Armstrong, his face aglow with wonder, lifts the lid and out pops Venetia dressed as a magician's assistant in tights and feathered head-dress. She is holding several old "Gina Gale" records with her picture on the sleeves

O'Toole and Armstrong help her out of the basket

O'Toole pushes the basket off stage

Venetia, posing and gesturing in time to the music, hands the records, one by one, to Armstrong

Venetia gives the audience a final flourish and a huge smile as she exits

Lights up on the living-room as Armstrong moves there. Armstrong's Light and the coloured Lights fade

(*Calling, excited*) Mum... Mum ... quick——
Pearl (*off*) I'm coming ... keep your hair on.

Pearl enters, dressed in her Sunday frock and sensible shoes—she carries her handbag

What is it now...?

Act I

Armstrong Look what I've found...
Pearl (*preoccupied, putting on lipstick*) What?
Armstrong I thought I'd give myself something to do—tidy up the attic...
Pearl (*still taking no interest*) How many times have I told you not to go up there, Armstrong. That's where *he* spent most of his time.
Armstrong Who's Gina Gale...?
Pearl (*ashen, sick to the stomach*) Who...?
Armstrong (*innocent, unaware*) Gina Gale—who was she?
Pearl Oh, my God! Where did you get them from...?
Armstrong I've just told you—are you going rotten deaf or what...?
Pearl (*landing him one about the head*) Don't you talk to me like that, lad, because I'll blind you...!
Armstrong (*shielding himself from her blows*) Mum ... what's up with you—I was only joking...!
Pearl You'd no right to touch that basket—no right at all. (*She grabs the records etc. from him*)
Armstrong They're only old records and some smelly film magazines...
Pearl (*screaming at him, hitting him with a magazine*) They're *him*, Armstrong—that's what they are—they're bloody well *him*!

Beryl enters in panic, tea towel in hand

Beryl Whatever's to do—what's wrong?
Armstrong (*still shielding his head*) She's gone mad, Beryl ... she's hitting me here...
Pearl (*giving Beryl the records etc.*) Take them, Beryl ... burn the buggers... I should have done it years ago...
Beryl Burn them ... why...?
Pearl Just do as I say—right! Get them out of my sight.
Beryl I don't know what he was doing up there in the first place—he knows it's out of bounds.

Beryl exits

Pearl (*almost breathless with fury*) Well, this has made a bugger of my bingo, hasn't it? The one night of the week I get to myself—the one night I can put my face on—get dressed up—and go with Gladys Greenhalgh to Empire bingo and enjoy myself. Well, that's put paid to that, hasn't it?

Armstrong (*almost in tears, hiding his face*) I don't see why. What've I done? I've never seen you like this before.
Pearl (*rounding on him again*) Don't ask what you've done, lad—because I'll thrash the arse off you!
Armstrong I'm sorry.
Pearl And don't say you're sorry because it won't wash—right? The times I've said do not go up into that loft—and what do you do when my back's turned? You deliberately defy me.
Armstrong I thought...
Pearl Yes, and you know what thought did! Have I been a bad mother to you or not?
Armstrong You haven't...
Pearl I must have been a good mother then.
Armstrong You have—you have been a good mother, Mum.
Pearl Right, well, in future, when I say don't do something (*she hits him again*) don't bloody well do it!
Armstrong (*shielding himself, terrified*) Mind me face, Mum ... me face...!
Pearl (*temper making her say things she shouldn't*) Your face, your face ... it's time you pulled yourself together, Armstrong. You'll be twenty next week—you're bone idle—you sit around here all day—and for what? There is nothing wrong with your face, Armstrong!

Beryl enters—nervous, worried

Beryl Mum—don't say that to him!
Pearl (*white with rage*) Well, I'm sick of it, Beryl. It's time we stopped pandering to him. (*She goes to Beryl and lifts Beryl's dress to show her leg*) This is what you call being a cripple! Look, Armstrong, look!
Beryl (*embarrassed*) Leave him, Mum.
Pearl (*putting on a coat and headscarf*) Yes, well, things have got to change round here. I'm not peeling onions all my sodding life. He's got to find a job, Beryl—it's time he started to support me in my old age!
Beryl You're not old, Mum...
Pearl (*still dressing to go out*) I soon will be at this rate. Now, I'm warning you, Armstrong—I'm off to bingo with Gladys Greenhalgh—and when I come back, and for ever more for that matter, I want no mention of your face. (*She goes to him, holding him by the shoulders*) Can you hear me or am I talking to that wall?

Act I   21

Armstrong (*avoiding her eyes, crying now, childlike*) Yes, Mum...
Pearl There is nothing wrong with your face—there's never been anything wrong with it—right?

No answer

(*Getting a hanky from her pocket*) Here—blow your nose.

He turns away from her, refusing to take the hanky

Please yourself. I've been far too soft with you, Armstrong. (*She goes to the exit*) I've been too soft with you both.

Pearl exits

Pause. We hear the front door slam

Armstrong (*temper and tears*) I'm going to kill her, Beryl... I am... I'm going to knife her!

Silence. He continues to cry, wiping his nose on his sleeve. Beryl just looks on looking upset

Beryl (*after a while, softly, gently*) It's no use crying, Armstrong.

He sits at the table, pulling at the sleeve of his pullover

That won't solve anything. (*Beat*) She didn't mean it. I'm sure she didn't mean it.
Armstrong (*crying, wiping his face on his shirt sleeve*) I've never seen her like that before.
Beryl No, well, she was upset.
Armstrong I don't know what I did wrong, Beryl.
Beryl It was the basket, love. She'd chosen to forget it even existed. (*Trying to comfort him*) And she didn't mean that about your birth-mark.
Armstrong I have got a birth-mark, haven't I, Beryl?
Beryl Yes, love—of course you have. But Mum wants everything to be perfect because it never has been. I'm surprised she even mentioned my

leg. She never has before. Oh yes—she mentioned it once—years ago—the day me dad left.
Armstrong (*innocently*) For Bangkok...?
Beryl I don't think he went to Bangkok, Armstrong. I think he was joking.
Armstrong Who was O'Toole...

Silence. Beryl doesn't answer

Who was O'Toole, Beryl?

A pool of Light comes up—warm, pinkish

> *O'Toole, now dressed in a bespangled evening jacket and carrying a hand microphone, walks into it calling out bingo numbers*

The Lights in the living-room fade

> *During the following, Pearl enters into the bingo light, bringing a chair on which she sits. She has her bag and a bingo card and is crossing out her winning numbers*

O'Toole Legs eleven—number eleven ... quack-quack ... two little ducks—twenty-two ... just one more—forty-four ... on its own ... number one!
Pearl (*excited, to her "friend"*) Bloody Nora, Gladys—I'm doing well here...!

O'Toole continues to call out with the flourish of a bingo caller, his fancy evening jacket catching the light

O'Toole Twenty one—the key of the door ... man alive—number five...!
Pearl Christ, Gladys—I can't believe it!
O'Toole Clickety-click—sixty-six...!
Pearl (*shouting out*) Yes! Come on, you bugger—just one more...! (*She closes her eyes, not daring to look*)
O'Toole I'm in heaven ... number seven...!
Pearl (*jumping up, screaming for joy*) Yes! Bingo! Housey-housey! It's me—over here—Pearl Armstrong! I've bloody well won!

They both peer out into the darkened auditorium as if seeing each other

Act I   23

O'Toole (*into his microphone*) And I think we have a winner, ladies and gentlemen ... but I'd better just check...

O'Toole freezes—so does Pearl, her bingo card held aloft. Lights up in the living-room where Beryl is handing the records back to Armstrong

Armstrong What's this?
Beryl (*childlike*) The records. I think you should have them.
Armstrong But she told you to burn them. She'll go mad.
Beryl Not if she doesn't find out. It can be our little secret.
Armstrong (*just as childlike, taking the records, holding them close*) Beryl ... d'you think we dare...?

They both freeze, hand to mouth, like two naughty school kids

Pearl (*calling out into the auditorium*) What d'you mean—you'd better check—are you suggesting I'm in the habit of cheating? Can you hear this, Gladys...? (*"Gladys" has obviously gone*) Gladys...?
O'Toole (*speaking to her now*) No, offence, Missus—but it's my job to check all so-called winning cards.
Pearl So-called! This is genuine, cock. I want my hundred quid—now!
O'Toole (*checking her card*) Sure—that seems to be fine. Now, Missus, if you come to my private office at the end of the session I'll get money out of the safe.
Pearl Why can't I have it straight away?
O'Toole Now, come along—you don't think I'd be foolish enough to stash large amounts of money about my person, do you? There's thieves about, Missus—rogues and bleeding vagabonds who'd have it off me in a flash.
Pearl (*worried, looking about*) Did you happen to see where my friend went...?
O'Toole Ahh—your friend, was she...?
Pearl What d'you mean—"was she"? (*She calls*) Gladys?
O'Toole It happens all the time in here—you win a hundred smackers on the bingo and your so-called best friend gets the hump. I mean, Mrs Armstrong—can I call you Mrs Armstrong?—Gladys Greenhalgh comes in here every night of the week and she's never won a light.
Pearl It's the first time I've ever won anything.
O'Toole Is that right? Now, perhaps, between us, we could do something about that.

Pearl (*concerned about the missing "Gladys"*) D'you think she's gone off me…?

O'Toole (*putting an arm around her*) Money, Pearl—I hope I can call you Pearl—money—especially other folks' money can do shocking things to people. (*He snuggles up closer*) Look, how about I treat you to a Guinness later—in the snug at the *Owld Cock and Trumpet* round the corner—what would you say to that?

Pearl (*aware of his wandering hands*) Oh no. I don't think so. I'd rather get home.

O'Toole Oh, come on, now … a tiny bit of pleasure never did anyone any harm—eh?

Pearl (*still stunned by events*) I can't get over that—she just walks out an' leaves me.

O'Toole Fair-weather friends, Pearl—you can live without them. (*He squeezes her waist*)

Pearl (*for spite perhaps*) All right—I'll have a Guinness with you. Why not? One Guinness won't do me any harm.

O'Toole That's a really sexy perfume you have on tonight, Pearl. Essence of Desire is it?

Pearl Essence of Onion, love. It's all the rage just at present.

They gaze into each other's eyes and remain frozen in time

"Gina Gale" begins to sing as Armstrong's Light comes up DR. *He is standing there, the record sleeve, which has the picture of "Gina Gale", held close to his breast—he listens for a while before speaking to the audience*

Armstrong I remember that night for so many reasons: it was the first time and, as it turned out, the only time she ever hit me. I suppose that in itself was significant enough to indicate that changes were on the way. But even more disturbing—it was the night she first brought *him* home—the first time we'd ever had a stranger in our house…

Beryl enters behind him—half afraid, half excited

Beryl She's brought a man home, Armstrong. A man.

Armstrong (*not listening, still to the audience*) But none of that seemed to matter at the time because the most amazing—the most wonderful thing had happened… I'd discovered Gina Gale! The light at the end of

Act I

the tunnel which my sister was always promising me—but which had never been switched on—suddenly was. And it was overwhelming...!

Cross-fade. Lights up fully on the living-room as Armstrong's Light fades

Beryl Did you hear what I said, Armstrong? She's brought home a stranger...

Pearl and O'Toole suddenly unfreeze, turn and become part of the scene. It is obvious that both have had too much to drink

Pearl What are you two up to...?
Beryl Nothing, Mum. (*She grabs the record sleeve from Armstrong*)

The music suddenly cuts out

We're not up to anything. Are we, Armstrong?

Armstrong covers the side of his face and looks away

Pearl Something's going on—you can't fool me.

Armstrong and Beryl continue to look at O'Toole who, like Pearl, has had too much to drink. Pearl's face is flushed

(*Feeling slightly awkward*) This is a friend of mine...
Beryl Did you win at the bingo?
Pearl (*lying*) No, I didn't. When do I ever win at bingo? (*To O'Toole*) This is our Beryl ... and this is our Armstrong.

O'Toole tries to focus on Beryl

O'Toole Hiya...
Beryl (*shyly*) Hallo, Mr...
Armstrong (*still shading his face*) Who's he? What does he want?
Pearl (*unsteady, removing her coat and headscarf*) Now, don't get lippy, Armstrong. I've had enough out of you tonight—right?
Armstrong I only asked who *he* was.
Pearl And I've said haven't I? He's a friend. We went and had a few drinks—that's all. I'm entitled to a drink, aren't I?

Armstrong He's pissed up. So are you.
Beryl (*sensing trouble*) I was just off to bed. I've got work in the morning. Good-night, Mr...?
O'Toole Oh, good-night, Miss ... good-night to you.

Beryl exits

Pearl (*to Armstrong*) What about you—isn't it your bedtime too?
Armstrong I can stop up if I want—it's a free country.
O'Toole What's up with him...?
Pearl Armstrong's a bit shy. (*Unsteadily she makes for the chair*) So is our Beryl. (*She sits*) We're all a bit shy in this house.
O'Toole Has the lad got a toothache? Is it a toothache you have, son...?
Pearl He's got a bad face. A scar. He worries about it—don't you, Armstrong? (*To O'Toole*) Perhaps you'd better go up. (*To Armstrong*) He's stopping the night. You don't mind, do you? Not that it's any of your business. He's nowhere to stay—his landlady's chucked him out.

No reply. She nods to O'Toole to go up

O'Toole Will it be OK, then? (*As he goes, unsteady on his feet*) Good-night, son. I hope your tooth's better in the morning.

O'Toole exits

Pearl (*calling to him*) First left at the top of the stairs—not right. We don't want you climbing into bed with our Beryl! (*She laughs*)

Silence

(*With a touch of guilt maybe*) He's bloody daft, he is. It'll only be for one night, Armstrong. One night only.
Armstrong I thought you were past all that.
Pearl What...?
Armstrong You heard. All that. I thought you were past it.
Pearl (*becoming angry*) Past all what? Past all what, Armstrong? A bit of company? Someone to have a laugh with—to talk to? Is that what you mean...?
Armstrong He's having you on. He just wants a cheap bed for the night. You're old enough to be his mother.

Act I   27

Pearl Do you want another good hiding? Is that what you want? And speak of what you know—right? Because you don't know about anything, Armstrong.

He turns to her, he is like a child again, not really understanding the ways of the world

Armstrong Will you shag him?
Pearl (*with a half smile at his innocence, fondly*) Come here.
Armstrong (*sulking, hiding his face*) I won't.
Pearl I said come here.
Armstrong (*slowly going to her*) What?
Pearl (*patting her knee*) Sit down.
Armstrong I'm not.
Pearl Sit, Armstrong.

He sits on her lap—she puts her arms around him as she would a child—the sight is quite touching

Look, I'm sorry I shouted at you earlier. Will that do?

No answer

And I didn't mean to hit you. I lost my temper, that's all. That bloody old basket! Why did I never chuck it out? I thought I'd forgotten all that—I thought he was gone forever. (*Beat*) I'm sorry.

No answer—he is still sulking

Look, Armstrong—things can't always be nice, you know. Life isn't like that.
Armstrong Things used to be nice.
Pearl When? It's not true, love. What round here has ever been nice? Perhaps you thought it was—perhaps—because you were still growing up you only imagined it was. And that's good. That's how it should be. But you're a man now and you've got to face up to things. I mean—I'm not saying things won't be nice for you—I hope they will be—but you've got to be ready—you've got to be prepared for things not to be.
Armstrong Such as what?
Pearl Oh, I don't know. There's nothing you can actually put your finger

on—but it's best not to expect too much. I did, you see. I did—and it was a mistake. I thought everything was going to be smashing—terrific—dead nonchalant.

Armstrong But it wasn't, you mean?

Pearl No, love. It wasn't.

Armstrong Did you not love Dad? Were you not in love with him?

Pearl Well ... yes. I was. Once. I think.

Armstrong You think!

Pearl Armstrong—don't go on about it. I'm doing my best to warn you, that's all. I care about you—I do, honestly I do. I care about you and I care about our Beryl ... but I can't go on shielding you forever. You've got to face it out there—stand up for yourself. Look at Beryl—she had her drawbacks—her handicap—but she's done all right for herself. She's got the library—and Mr Gunter—and she doesn't expect me to protect her any longer.

Armstrong But Beryl's not happy.

Pearl I know. I know she's not. But she's learned to make the best of things. It's like I said earlier—she's like me—she's content.

Armstrong What does that mean—content?

Pearl It's when you've accepted second best—when you've come to terms with life—when you know that what you've got now is all you're ever going to get.

Armstrong When you've given up, you mean?

Pearl Well, it's not quite as bad as that, love. But you've got the gist.

Armstrong (*rising, moving down stage*) Was *he* like that, then? Was he unhappy?

Pearl I don't want to discuss it, Armstrong.

Armstrong I want to know. Was he unhappy?

Pearl To be fair to him—yes—I think he was unhappy. But he was a coward—he ran away. It was me who had to stop on and face the music. And I don't think I'm a martyr or that I feel sorry for myself—not all the time anyway—but somebody's got to stay behind—shoulder the burden—carry on as if everything was lovely...

Venetia enters from "out of the scene", dressed as "Gina Gale" again and smoking

Venetia (*fed up with all this*) Oh, do come on. This is getting very maudlin. Far too soppy. (*To the audience*) Don't you think?

Pearl (*furiously*) You jealous little madam. (*To Armstrong*) She's just ruined that bit—ruined it entirely!

Act I

Venetia You've been at it for ages. I want my turn. These poor people are fidgeting.
Pearl Fidgeting! Did she say...? You could have heard a pin drop out there.
Venetia I know. I thought they'd all gone home!
Armstrong Pack it in—both of you. We'll get to you in a minute, Venetia.
Venetia Yes, but when? It's dead boring sitting back there. (*To the audience*) I mean—you could smoke yourself silly!
Armstrong (*handing Pearl her coat and props etc.*) OK—we'll move on a bit—we'll get to her bits.
Venetia Shall I get ready?
Armstrong Go on, then.
Venetia (*to the audience*) You'll love my bits—they're really dramatic!

Venetia exits—excited

Pearl What about me—have I finished or what?
Armstrong For the minute, yes. I want to move on.
Pearl This isn't how it happened, Armstrong—you know that.
Armstrong It's how I want it to happen—right? I'm in charge here.
Pearl Could I just suggest...?
Armstrong (*glaring at her*) Who's writing this? Just go!

Pearl, obviously afraid of him, exits

The living-room Lights fade as Armstrong's Light comes up. Getting back into character he walks over to it

(*Alone in his light, to the audience*) Mum never mentioned money again after that night—and what was even more surprising—she gave up her job peeling onions. The Irishman moved in permanently and slept up in her bed. But at least they were out at bingo every night—and somehow—don't ask me how—she was always winning. I kept my mouth shut—so did our Beryl. And as for Mum—well, it was Babylon revisited ... for a while anyway.

"Gina Gale" starts to sing

During the singing, Venetia enters and places a bench, which will act as two cinema seats, DC. *She has a packet of Butterkist popcorn. She sits*

Soft Lights come up around her as she eats her Butterkist. Armstrong walks over and stands behind her as he addresses the audience. His Light fades

> I still went to the pictures—once a week—on a Tuesday—but always on my own now. Mum was usually out with Gobshite and our Beryl did as much overtime as she could—just to be near Cyril Gunter.

The "Gina Gale" song fades and is taken over by soft cinema music

> I'd creep in trying not to let people see my face—and I'd always sit on my own... On that particular night however... I didn't. (*He sits beside Venetia—a hand up to his face*)
> **Venetia** (*after a while*) It'll be the adverts next—then the big picture. (*Beat*) I have seen it before, actually—twice—but I love it so much—especially the end where they meet on that hill and she tells him it's her who's done the murder and he turns out not to be her uncle at all, but a man from the FBI. (*She continues to stuff popcorn into her mouth*)
> **Armstrong** Yeah. (*He takes another sly look at her*) Hey, haven't I seen you somewhere before?
> **Venetia** Here—just you watch it—right?
> **Armstrong** Sorry...?
> **Venetia** I've met your sort in here before. Well, I know the manager, right, and one word from me and you'll be out on your ear.
> **Armstrong** Oh. I see. Right.
> **Venetia** If your hand so much as touches my leg once these lights have gone down—well—I'm just warning you, that's all.
> **Armstrong** (*puzzled by all this*) Oh, right. (*He pauses and takes another sidelong glance at her*) I'm sorry—but has anyone ever told you...?
> **Venetia** (*suspicious*) Told me what?
> **Armstrong** Oh nothing. (*Beat*) It's just that you bear a striking resemblance to Gina Gale.
> **Venetia** Gina Gale? (*Beat*) Who's Gina Gale when she's at home?
> **Armstrong** She sings. She's a star.
> **Venetia** (*impressed now*) Really. A film star?
> **Armstrong** Well, not actually a film star—but a star just the same.
> **Venetia** Oh, I see. I'm thinking of becoming a star.
> **Armstrong** You've got the same hair an' everything. The same mouth. The same lip-gloss. Do you sing?

Act I 31

Venetia Well, I did at school. Mr Popplewell said that with very intensive training—every night like—he could get me on the stage proper an' that.
Armstrong You see—I knew it.
Venetia He offered to give me private lessons an' everything. For free.
Armstrong Did you go?
Venetia No. Me mam wouldn't let me. She'd heard what his singing lessons were like!

Silence

Armstrong Can I get you a lolly? A choc-ice?
Venetia No, thanks. (*Beat*) Would you like a Butterkist?

She offers her bag—he takes some

Here—what's wrong with your face?
Armstrong (*hand to his face since he has been talking to her*) It's very badly scarred. I've had it since I was born. A birthmark.
Venetia (*fascinated, almost envious*) Really? Can I see it? I love birth marks.
Armstrong Gerroff...!
Venetia No, I do, honest. Come on—let me see it. If you show me yours I'll show you mine. I promise I won't laugh.

Slowly, he removes his hand—she peers closely at his face

There's nothing there.
Armstrong Sorry...?
Venetia You're mad—there's nothing there. You've got a very nice face.
Armstrong (*touched, warming to her at once*) No-one's ever said that to me before.
Venetia Well, you have. What's your name?
Armstrong Armstrong. Armstrong Armstrong. It's daft, isn't it?
Venetia It's not daft. It's quite catchy actually. Mine's Venetia. Venetia De La Bastide. (*Beat*) Do I really look like what's-her-name?
Armstrong Exactly like her.
Venetia Do you know her personally? Could you get me an introduction?
Armstrong I don't know her at all. I'm just in love with her, that's all. I have written to her though ... several times.

Venetia (*impressed*) Did she reply?
Armstrong I never sent them. I don't know where she lives. I have made enquiries, but nobody seems to know where she lives.

She looks slightly wary now—could this man be a loony perhaps?

Here ... you said you'd show me yours.
Venetia (*alarmed*) What...?
Armstrong You know. Your birthmark.
Venetia I can't—you daft thing. Not in here. It's in a rather private place. Have you got a girlfriend?
Armstrong No. (*Beat*) I've been too busy.
Venetia I see. Oh, it's about to start.

The House Lights in the "cinema" go down as the background music fades and the flicker from the "screen" starts

Armstrong (*lowering his voice*) If you like ... one day ... when you've got a free moment ... you can come round to our house and I'll show you a picture of her.
Venetia Really? (*Beat, looking up at the "screen"*) A picture of who?
Armstrong (*also looking up at the "screen"*) Gina. I've got all her records. Me dad left them to me. In his will.
Venetia Well, I'll have to think about it.
Armstrong (*disappointed*) Oh.
Venetia It doesn't do to rush things.

She gives him one of her smiles

Armstrong.

They look up at the "screen" together

Slowly, very slowly, we see their hands growing ever closer until they touch—she squeezes his hand gently—his face is now aglow. Loudly, thrillingly, "Gina Gale" begins to sing. Armstrong rises and runs across to R where his Light comes up brightly. The song suddenly cuts out

Armstrong (*overwhelmed, thrilled, close to tears of joy*) Hey, I walked her home ... all the way ... straight to her door ... I even bought her some chips! We arranged to meet again the following Tuesday ... and the

Act I

Tuesday after that! (*He hugs himself with delight*) Isn't she beautiful...? Venetia! I've never known anyone called Venetia before. Venetia De La Bastide! Sounds a bit foreign—don't you think...? And she said I had a nice face—did you hear that? No-one's ever said that to me before. Well, that's it—my mind's made up... (*He shades his eyes from the light and calls out into the dark auditorium*) Gina...? Gina...? Are you there, Gina...? I'm in love. I mean really in love. It doesn't mean I think any the less of you, Gina—but I'm going to marry Venetia... Venetia De La Bastide!

O'Toole, dressed once again in his dark suit and smoking a cigarette, appears from the gloom beyond the light and comes to stand directly behind Armstrong, half in, half out of his light

Armstrong's face changes now to a look of terror. Slow fade to Black-out

ACT II

In the darkness, "Gina Gale" begins to sing an up-beat number: first verse in darkness; second verse—a single spot comes up on "Gina Gale", motionless and with her back to us. During the middle section, the Light DR *comes up slightly as Pearl, Beryl and O'Toole take their places. Last verse—"Gina Gale" becomes animated, miming to the record etc. Slowly she turns to us and we see it is Armstrong dressed in Venetia's Act I clothes, her blonde wig, make-up, lip-gloss, etc. The song ends—we hear the sound of rapturous applause and cheering. Armstrong, overcome with emotion, blows kisses and bows lovingly to his audience*

The Light on Pearl, Beryl and O'Toole comes up more intensely. Pearl, as if confronted by a ghost, screams out in horror as her hand flies to her mouth. Armstrong, suddenly transfixed, frozen in horror at having been caught like this

Armstrong (*out front, as if addressing his mother*) Mum, Mum... I didn't expect you home!
Pearl (*crying out*) My God! It's history ... repeating itself...!

Armstrong, in panic, tearing off the wig, runs off stage as the single spot fades

Softly, distantly, "Gina Gale" starts to sing Who's Sorry Now

Venetia joins the group down stage. She has taken on the Armstrong family look of Act I: quite plain without her make-up and blonde wig—she wears a simple cotton frock, her dull, straight hair held in place with a plastic hair-slide

Pearl looks older now, pale and shabby in a headscarf and an unbecoming mac, a dirty canvas shopping bag over her arm. Beryl, too, looks more mature and quite smart in a two-piece grey suit with matching hat and gloves. O'Toole, sitting on the high stool, is once more dressed in his

Act II

glittering bingo-caller's evening jacket. After a suitable pause, Venetia speaks to the audience, quieter now—disillusioned. Music fades

Venetia I married Armstrong on my twenty-first birthday. It pissed down. The cake didn't arrive. The vicar got lost and turned up half an hour late. (*Beat*) I suppose I should have known then that it was some kind of omen. Not that I would have taken any notice—not that I would have been able to do anything about it. It was too late. Well, I mean, you've plighted your troth or whatever they call it. You can hardly go back and say you've changed your mind, can you? I knew after a fortnight it was a disaster. Not that we hadn't—well, you know—we had *done* it an' everything—the consecration an' all that. Whatever Armstrong's deficiencies are he's not impotent. But, well ... well, it wasn't quite what they'd cracked it up to be. I mean, you hear such stories, don't you? About "the earth moving" and "making lovely music" and all that. Not that we went short of music, mind—but it's not easy trying to make love to an old Gina Gale record, is it? And he had to have it on loud ... very loud in fact. That's why we usually only did it when Beryl was late at the library and his mother was out at bingo with what's-his-face. At least we had the house to ourselves. But then we'd have the neighbours knocking on the wall and shouting, "Turn that friggin' noise down!" You know—how they do.

Pause. She wipes her nose with a hanky

So, you see—all in all—I'm not happy.

Venetia attempts a half smile—then walks away into the darkness beyond the light

Beryl (*to the audience*) I don't know whether you heard, but Mr Gunter died. He died. Suicide actually. "While the balance of his mind was disturbed" was how they worded it. It was me who found him. He'd hanged himself from one of the old beams at the library. I haven't got over it yet... I don't think I ever shall. He'd been caught, you see ... caught by the police in a lavatory in Jubilee Park. His name was in all the papers and he was due to appear in court on the Tuesday as I found him on the Monday. (*Beat*) I suppose it was all too much for him. (*Beat*) It's his mother I feel sorry for.

Beryl, too, walks away into the darkness

Pearl (*to the audience*) They gave me three months. The magistrate said he would have given me longer, but as it was my first offence and I'd obviously been led up the garden he felt he should be lenient. He said I was a silly and foolish middle-aged woman, trying to recapture her youth, who had fallen under the spell of a common and ruthless criminal. Youth? What youth...?

O'Toole (*twinkle in his eye*) Sure—I thought it was a great idea. It was. It was a bloody wonderful idea. And it might have worked if that spiteful owld cow Gladys Greenhalgh hadn't cottoned on an' split on us. (*He lights a cigarette*) I'd worked it all out ... very fastidiously ... on bits o' paper an' everything. I reckoned that if Pearl here won on the bingo—say at least once a fortnight—we could share the proceeds fifty-fifty like——

Pearl (*to him, angry*) Fifty-fifty! Come off it—seventy-thirty more like.

O'Toole (*as if she hadn't spoken at all*) —Now, what I was aiming at was the big one ... once every six weeks we had what you call the accumulator. The bonanza. The jackpot! Three thousand nicker in your hand with a friggin' security guard to see you home, like! (*He drags on his fag*) And we did it. No sweat. I knew the numbers on her card, d'you see? And as I was in sole charge of selecting the bingo balls—well, you can guess the rest. I mean, somebody had to win it. It was a fucking cinch...! She called "bingo", I looked surprised—sure, it's all part of the act in my line—I got somebody else to check her card just to add a touch of verisimilitude—and that was it! We paid her out the money and she stuffed it in her handbag—up her jumper—down her drawers—every-bloody-where ... and what happens? (*He drags on his fag*) We get outside an' the cops is waiting. Jesus! Talk about shittin' yourself. Like I said—Gladys Greenhalgh had shopped us—otherwise—on the Pope's death (*he crosses himself*) we'd have got away with it. (*He rises*) I got two years—two years! Again!

He gives us a wry smile and walks away into the darkness taking the stool with him

The sound of "Gina Gale" singing Who's Sorry Now *returns*

Pearl is left alone. As her Light begins to fade, the Lights come up on the living-room. We notice the typewriter is set on the table—a sheet of paper

Act II

in it ready to be typed upon. Pearl enters the living-room looking tired, older, weary. She looks about the room as if seeing it for the first time and not liking what she sees

Pearl Look at it. Hide-away Hall. (*She sits at the table*)

The music fades

Armstrong enters, dressed again in his own clothes, but with the make-up only half removed—a dirty towel in his hands. He slowly goes across to his mother and attempts to kiss her on the cheek

She puts a hand up to stop him

Don't, Armstrong. Just don't—right?

The scene is played slowly, quietly

Armstrong I didn't expect you. I didn't know you were coming out. Why didn't you let us know?
Pearl I thought it'd be a surprise. I'll surprise 'em, I thought. Some bloody surprise—what?
Armstrong Shall I put the kettle on?
Pearl I shouldn't bother. (*Beat*) So. How long's this been going on, then?
Armstrong (*playing the innocent*) What?
Pearl You know, Armstrong. Don't be acting gormless. All this. Dressing up in a tart's frock—wearing make-up.
Armstrong I only do it here. When I'm on my own. I don't go to Tesco's in it.
Pearl It's not right, Armstrong. Doing it on your own doesn't make it right, lad. In fact it makes it worse. (*To heaven*) Honestly, what have I done to deserve all this? First his dad—the twat—now him! "Oh, just to get home", I thought, "just to get home where everything's normal". Normal!
Armstrong Everything *is* normal, Mum. Nothing's changed.
Pearl Where's our Beryl? I suppose she's blacking up and doing Al Jolson impressions!
Armstrong There's no need to be sarcastic. She's out.
Pearl And her—where's she?

Armstrong Venetia's at work.
Pearl And you? What about you, Armstrong—did you find a job?
Armstrong Well, I er…
Pearl Yes or no?
Armstrong No.
Pearl What were your last words to me? As they carted me off in that Black Maria, what did you say, Armstrong? "I'll get a job, Mum", you cried. "I'll get a good job and buy a new carpet for the living-room". (*She looks down at the carpet*) It's still here I see.

Long silence. He sits in the armchair—on the edge—his knees together— the dirty towel still in his hands

Armstrong (*at length*) How was it?
Pearl Oh, it was very nice, Armstrong—lovely. You want to try it sometime.
Armstrong We didn't tell anybody. We just kept it to ourselves. If anybody asked we said you'd gone on your holidays.
Pearl Holidays! Holidays? For three months? It was in all the papers, Armstrong.
Armstrong Yes, but not everybody read it, Mum.
Pearl You live in a world of your own, Armstrong. But then you always did. Gladys would have seen to it that they all read the papers. (*Beat. She wipes her face on her headscarf*) You never wrote. Our Beryl never wrote.
Armstrong You told us not to.
Pearl Yes, but I didn't mean it, Armstrong… I didn't mean it.
Armstrong Well, how were we to know you didn't mean it?
Pearl Don't get lippy—right? Don't get lippy, Armstrong—because the mood I'm in I'm just as likely to go mad and wipe this friggin' floor with you! (*From her pocket she produces a crumpled bag of boiled sweets and pops one in her mouth. She offers him the bag*) D' you want a toffee?
Armstrong (*sulking*) No, thanks.
Pearl (*putting them away*) Please yourself. (*Beat*) I'm very disappointed, Armstrong, I hope you know that. (*She sucks her sweet*) Very disappointed.
Armstrong I did try to get a job—I did—honest. I queued up an' everything. "Nothing today", she'd say, so I'd go in tomorrow and the day after that, but the message was always the same… "Nothing today!"

Act II

She asked me if I'd considered a re-training scheme. "Re-training?" I said... "I never trained for anything in the first place..." "When did you last work?" she said. It was embarrassing. "I've never worked at all", I said, and she called the manager. "We've got a right case here, Mr Duckinfield", she said, "this young man's been idle since he left Dorothy Street Secondary!" she said. Everybody was skennin' at me... I felt that small... "What do you do with yourself all day?" he said. "Mawl about or what?"

Pearl "No, I dress up in my wife's clothes and pretend to be some tart who used to sing!" Is that what you told him?

Armstrong Gina Gale was not a tart!

Pearl I suppose them were *his* records?

No answer

Well?

No answer

I see. I've been betrayed on all sides. I expressly told our Beryl to burn them buggers. You've had 'em all this time...? (*Beat—shouting*) Answer me, Armstrong!

Armstrong (*shielding his head in case she attacks*) Yes. I hid 'em... I've only ever played them when you were out.

Pearl What a life, eh? What a bloody life! I'd be better off inside—I would. I've a good mind to catch the next bus and go back—"Let me in!" I shall cry at them gates—"Let me come back!"—and they would, Armstrong. If I told them only half the heartbreak you and our Beryl have caused me they'd have me back like a shot! There's a woman in there—chopped up her husband and put him down the lav—and she's not half as daft as you!

Armstrong I'm not daft.

Pearl You're daft, Armstrong. Take my word for it. You were born daft—you've remained daft—and you always will be daft! Is there a funny smell in here?

Armstrong I don't think so.

Pearl My nostrils are very sensitive—there's a definite smell in this house. I suppose you never wash your socks. Never wash up. I'll bet that bottle of Fairy Liquid hasn't been touched since I left this house.

Armstrong It has.

Silence. Pearl sighs—world-weary

Pearl Well, I don't know what I'm going to do and that's a fact. I went to rehabilitation, but she was no help. "How can I hold my head up?" I asked her. "How can I look my neighbours in the face?" She couldn't answer. "What's it like at home?" she said, "have you got a stable and loving home environment?" "No", I said—"I live in a madhouse with a disabled daughter and a social misfit for a son!" That woman wept, Armstrong—right there—in that office—that woman broke her heart for me. (*Beat*) You're not listening, are you?
Armstrong It's all *his* fault. You should never have got entangled with him.
Pearl I know that now, don't I? I know that now, Armstrong. My life went out that window the night you found that basket.
Armstrong Oh, so you're blaming it on me now.

She lifts her arm

I'm sorry, I didn't mean it.

Silence. Pearl wipes her face again

Beryl's joined the Church of the Ubiquitous Saints.
Pearl (*thinking she's misheard*) She's what...?
Armstrong Beryl. Cyril Gunter topped himself—our Beryl became depressed—lost the point of everything—she met this chap who'd been had-up for flashing, but had seen the error of his ways and turned to Jesus. Beryl's joined him.
Pearl I don't believe it. I do not believe it. I turn my back for five minutes...!
Armstrong She's given up the library. It held too many memories for her.
Pearl So what does she do all day—how does she earn her living?
Armstrong She goes out with him ... knocking on doors ... spreading the message.
Pearl What message?
Armstrong I don't think she knows.
Pearl And what about money? We need money to exist, Armstrong. We get none from you.
Armstrong People give them a donation just to get rid of them. They bring it back here and share it out.

Act II

Pearl (*to heaven*) Oh, my God ... where's it all going to end ... what will the harvest be?
Armstrong It's Gobshite. (*He picks up his manuscript*) That's what I've called him. Our Beryl's under his spell—mesmerized. (*He holds the manuscript to his chest*) They're out all day and in bed all night ... counting their takings and praying.
Pearl In bed? Here? Our Beryl?
Armstrong At least she's happy. More than can be said for us.
Pearl And whose fault's that? I did tell you. I did warn you, Armstrong—but would you listen—would you take the slightest bit of notice?
Armstrong (*his mind seems to be elsewhere*) I've been doing a lot of thinking since you've been away. I think I should kill Venetia. I mean—what use is she?
Pearl Now—we don't want any of that sort of talk, Armstrong—right?
Armstrong But I could make it quick. Painless. I could push her down a manhole—out of a train...
Pearl When do you ever go on a train—talk sense.
Armstrong A quick slash with the bread knife, then. I could even poison her Horlicks.
Pearl I'm not listening, Armstrong. Poor cow—you've only been together five minutes.
Armstrong Yes, but she's not the woman I married, Mum. (*He puts the manuscript down on the table*) She's changed. She's no longer carefree—she's very slipshod about her appearance—she doesn't even clean her teeth any more when she comes to bed.
Pearl What about your conjugal rights?
Armstrong Up the Swanee. She just turns over and says "bollocks". And all those nice clothes she used to wear—the blonde wig—just cast aside.
Pearl Does she know you wear them?
Armstrong (*throwing up his arms in frustration*) I just want to change things—put everything right.
Pearl (*shouting*) Well, you can't! Life is life. And nobody can change it. We'd like to change it—we'd love to change it—but we can't!

Beat. His eyes are now aglow with excitement

Armstrong I could. I could do it.
Pearl (*suspiciously*) How?

Armstrong With this. (*He indicates the typewriter*) All I need is this and my imagination.
Pearl And where did that come from?
Armstrong I got it second hand on the market. It's all I've ever wanted, Mum.
Pearl Oh, my God! Listen to him. You've got to work, Armstrong. Work, love.
Armstrong This'll be my work. Can't you see? I can just lock myself away here and be creative.
Pearl Resist it, Armstrong. In God's name resist it. Try to be ordinary—for my sake—try to be commonplace.
Armstrong But we've got to face facts, Mum. I'm not ordinary, am I? I'm not commonplace. I'm destined for higher things. For Bangkok!
Pearl (*to the audience*) You see—what did I tell you? This is his dad talking.
Armstrong (*standing on a chair, reaching out*) That's what will make me famous, Mum. Famous like I've always wanted. At last I shall be a "somebody". Who knows—an OBE. A Nobel Prize. A touch on the shoulder with a sword. "Arise, Sir Armstrong Armstrong—Oxon!"
Pearl (*to the audience*) It's in the sperm—that's what it is. Whatever a father passes on to his son is in the sperm. This is what comes of fornication!
Armstrong Don't mention fornication to me. (*Madness in his eyes now, he jumps down from the chair*) I'm never going to fuck again—ever!
Pearl The day his dad left, I thought, that's it, I thought—now I've finally landed on my feet, I thought. But he might as well be back—he's the spitting image of him!
Armstrong (*tearfully*) Help me, Mum. Please help me.
Pearl (*touched by him now*) Armstrong...?
Armstrong (*quietly*) I need to do something, Mum... I can't go on much longer.
Pearl (*anxiously*) What d'you mean?
Armstrong I might do what me dad did. I might just run away.
Pearl Oh not that. Not that, Armstrong. How would I manage?
Armstrong But what is there? There's no pleasure any more ... life's become humdrum ... run of-the-mill ... uneventful. (*He turns to look at her, childlike again, lost*) Just like you predicted.
Pearl (*helplessly*) Don't, Armstrong—don't be like this.
Armstrong Mr Lumsworthy was right. I'm a wanker.

Act II

Pearl You're not, love. Come here.

No answer

Have a toffee, eh? (*She offers the bag*) Come on.

He goes to her, crestfallen, takes a toffee and puts it in his mouth. She pats her lap, he sits on it, his arm around her shoulder. Madonna and child

(*Trying to cheer him up*) I spoil you, you know. I do. And I'm going to live to regret it. (*She holds him tight, kisses and ruffles his hair*)
Armstrong Am I useless?
Pearl Course you're not useless. Not to me at any rate. You're my little precious, aren't you? So's our Beryl—bless her. (*Beat. A thought strikes her*) The Church of the what...?
Armstrong (*his head on her shoulder*) Ubiquitous Saints. (*Beat. Thumb in mouth now*) I'm glad you're home. I've missed you...

The sound of a typewriter is heard—the pounding of the keyboard—the ping of its bell. Cross-fade of Lighting—down on the living-room—Lights up DL

Beryl limps on, dressed in her smart two-piece with handbag and hat to match. O'Toole enters and stands directly behind her—he now looks shabby in a huge brown overcoat and thick pebble glasses. Each carries a Bible. She reaches out to ring a "door bell"

The sound of a door bell

Beryl (*as the "door" is opened*) Oh, good-afternoon. My friend and I have a message for you ... it's a message from Jesus... Blessed are the meek, sayeth the Lord, for it is they who shall inherit the earth. We're in the vicinity today to tell all our friends the good news... He's coming back ... it could be tomorrow—it could be next week—we might even have to wait till next year—but He's on his way. Now, what do you think about that? Isn't it wonderful? (*She awaits a reply—but nothing*) Will you shun Him or will you throw open your heart and welcome Him in? (*Beat*) What do you think He will say when He arrives? Will He be amazed by all the changes that have taken place while He's been away or do you think He really knows? Perhaps God the Father will have kept him in touch ... hmmm? *(From her bag she produces a home-made newsletter)* Perhaps you'd like to read through our pamphlet—"Trumpets for the Lord" ... It's fifty pence or whatever you would care to donate. It all goes to charity. We've already given two million to the babies in Mozambique...

The "door" is obviously slammed shut in her face

That wasn't very nice...!
O'Toole And bollocks to you, mate! Fear not, Beryl. Some of them are ignorant bastards.
Beryl What appalling behaviour...
O'Toole "Forgive them for they know not what they do."
Beryl *(upset, blowing her nose)* We're beset by Philistines and heathens.
O'Toole The other cheek, Beryl—always remember the other cheek, dear.
Beryl I don't think I'm cut out for this caper. I'm no better than a door-to-door salesperson offering a product nobody wants.
O'Toole *(an arm on her shoulder)* Take a deep breath now—a deep breath and put it out of your mind.

She tries to smile

How about a quick one—a quick one in *The Frog and Tulip*—a small port and lemon—a packet of cheese and onion—it often works wonders, Beryl.
Beryl *(taking his clammy hand)* Yes. You're right. As usual.

Softly, at a distance, "Gina Gale" begins to sing Who's Sorry Now. *O'Toole, looking very sinister now in his long overcoat and pebble glasses, places one hand on Beryl's breast. She looks down fearfully at the hand so intimately placed*

Armstrong's Light comes up DR *as Venetia steps into it*

Another powerful shaft of Light comes up C *on Armstrong still sitting on Pearl's knee*

(Distressed, calling out across time and distance into the dark audito-

Act II   45

rium) Armstrong…? Armstrong—are you there? I'm not happy, Armstrong. I'm not happy like this. I was much happier with Mr Gunter and with things the way they should be… Mr Gunter and I had so much in common…

O'Toole (*softly, seductively*) Shall we go home now, Beryl, dear … would you like that? Straight home and straight to bed … now wouldn't you like that? (*He fondles her breast*) Sure—I know you would.

Beryl winces as she catches his bad breath

Beryl Please, Armstrong … enough now … please put everything right.
Venetia (*calling out urgently*) He's mad … he is. Friggin' stark-staring. He should be put away … out of it … locked up before he takes over our lives. They're scared of him—but I'm not. And he loves it—he knows that when people are afraid of you—you can do anything!

The Light on the smiling Armstrong grows even brighter as Pearl bounces him on her lap and begins to sing If You're Happy and You Know It. *The "Gina Gale" song fades away as Pearl's voice takes over. After the first eight lines are sung, Beryl, Venetia and O'Toole join in the song with an almost evangelical fervour as they set about transforming the stage back to how it was at the start of the play. Everything disappears—the floral book-flat returns to its plain black state—furniture is hidden away from where it came until we are back as we began*

   Pearl, Beryl and Venetia exit, still singing until their voices trail away to nothing

Silence. Armstrong pounds away at his typewriter. O'Toole, dressed again in his dark suit, sits on the bench, smoking and reading Armstrong's manuscript. The stage is lit by harsh pools of white Light

O'Toole (*having finished the last page*) It doesn't end. (*Beat. He looks across at Armstrong*) How does it finish?
Armstrong Who knows?
O'Toole You must have some idea.
Armstrong I don't. That's half the fun. In death perhaps.
O'Toole That's a pity. Whose?
Armstrong Haven't decided. Armstrong's?

O'Toole Too easy. He needs help—not to be killed off.
Armstrong (*stopping work*) Who says *he* needs help?
O'Toole Maybe I've misunderstood—I'm sorry.
Armstrong The mother, the daughter, the wife. It's they who need help. Maybe I'll kill one of them. (*He is trying out a word on paper with a pencil*) How the hell do you spell ubiquitous?
O'Toole (*reading*) Sorry...?
Armstrong Are you deaf or what? Ubiquitous. (*His pencil breaks*) Bugger!
O'Toole It's a good word. It means ever present ... everywhere ... often encountered ... in several places simultaneously.
Armstrong (*sharpening his pencil with a knife*) I know all that—I'm a writer—I want to know how you spell it.
O'Toole (*rapidly*) U-B-I-Q-U-I-T-O-U-S. Ubiquitous! I suspect that is your favourite word. No? My favourite word is "serendipity". Now, serendipity is a beautiful word.
Armstrong Oh, yeah ... fancy that.
O'Toole And what about solipsism? Now solipsism is a wonderful word. "Solipsist" as a noun; "solipsistic", the adjective. It describes Armstrong awfully well.
Armstrong (*head in hands*) I am trying to work. How can I work with you parroting on and on?
O'Toole I'm sorry. Please carry on.

Armstrong tries to continue, but once again has become irritable, rips the paper from the machine and throws it aside—rises and moves about—on edge

Armstrong You see. You've done it again. I've become ... become...
O'Toole (*as if to irritate him further*) Pugnacious? Belligerent? Quarrelsome—out of sorts?
Armstrong (*cracking, covering his head, crying out*) Bollocks! Bollocks! Bollocks!
O'Toole A taboo word meaning testicles, I believe.

Armstrong lies on the floor in an effort to calm down and relax—he breathes deeply

Armstrong You'll wear me down—you know that, don't you? You'll crush me eventually. I'll become like Armstrong—defeated.
O'Toole Is he? Is Armstrong defeated?

Act II

Armstrong Nearly. Very nearly. But he'll fight back. He usually does. (*Arms behind his head now, more relaxed*) What is this place anyway?
O'Toole (*suddenly paying particular attention, rising*) Which place?
Armstrong (*tired, eyes closed*) This. This place. What is it?
O'Toole (*standing over him, looking down*) It's just a place. It's whatever place you want it to be.
Armstrong It's not home. I know that much. Home's much nicer than this.
O'Toole You think so?
Armstrong (*suddenly sitting up, at O'Toole's feet*) And you. Who are you? You come here every day—read my work when I'd rather you didn't—say nothing—then leave. Are you a critic?

O'Toole smiles to himself

Perhaps you're a warder.
O'Toole I'm not a warder. This isn't a prison.
Armstrong You're a doctor. Is that it?
O'Toole Is that what you'd like—would you like me to be a doctor?

Silence

Armstrong What's your name again?
O'Toole You know my name. You've used it a thousand times.
Armstrong Well, whatever your name is I think you're a fake. A charlatan. An impostor. And you're Irish.
O'Toole Sadly—that's a fact.
Armstrong I don't like the Irish. They expose themselves to innocent bystanders. Flash their dicks and run away. Bring chaos where once there was calm.

O'Toole laughs pleasantly and lights another cigarette

Why do you laugh all the time?
O'Toole Because I think you're funny. At least *some* of the time you're funny.
Armstrong You shouldn't smoke. It's bad for you.
O'Toole (*enjoying his cigarette*) So they say.
Armstrong (*jumping to his feet*) Can I have one? I suddenly fancy it.
O'Toole Of course. (*He holds out the packet*)

Armstrong takes a cigarette—O'Toole lights it for him. For a strange, almost intimate moment the two men gaze into each other's eyes

Armstrong (*staring at O'Toole*) Solip—what...?
O'Toole (*staring at him*) Sism. Solipsism.
Armstrong Meaning...?
O'Toole It's a term used by philosophers. It means taking the view that "self" is all that exists or all that can be known.

Armstrong, looking away, thinks about this for a moment, then looks back at O'Toole

Armstrong That there is nothing beyond oneself, then?
O'Toole Sort of—ish.
Armstrong Selfish? Self-centred? Self-loving?
O'Toole (*wary*) Perhaps.
Armstrong Worse than that?
O'Toole Not worse. Different.
Armstrong Much?

O'Toole makes a gesture to mean so-so

(*Moving away now*) And you think that describes me?
O'Toole I didn't say that. I said it described Armstrong quite well. In your story—at least how you've written him—he has a tendency to shut everything out. Things which truly are: things ... places ... people. No?
Armstrong Maybe. He doesn't always manage it, though. What happens then?
O'Toole He's your invention. You tell me.
Armstrong I'm asking you, for Christ's sake—you seem to understand him better than me.
O'Toole (*turning away himself now*) Perhaps then he attempts to distort that which cannot be shut out. Change what really exists into something that doesn't. Fact becomes fiction. (*He turns and looks across at Armstrong*) Or fantasy even. People like Armstrong can often be unhappy with the truth so they alter it—re-arrange it to suit themselves. It makes life more bearable—easier to endure. It's more common than you'd think. But it can be dangerous—it can get out of hand.
Armstrong Oh?

Act II   49

O'Toole That's when you need help. Or at least when Armstrong needs it.

They stare at each other for a moment

Armstrong You're so fucking clever, aren't you! Did you study philosophy, then—is that it?
O'Toole Only on a modest scale.
Armstrong And madness. Did you study that on a modest scale also?

No answer

I'm not enjoying this cigarette.
O'Toole Then put it out. Extinguish it.

Without taking his eyes off the other man, Armstrong drops his cigarette to the floor and steps on it. O'Toole, after a moment, does the same. Armstrong then goes over to the bench, sits and picks up the manuscript

Armstrong So. I suppose I'd better ask. What do you make of all this? Do you like my work? Do you think I can make it?

O'Toole simply smiles

You can be honest. I'm not afraid of the truth.
O'Toole (*amused slightly*) One must first admit that truth exists before one can be afraid of it.
Armstrong You're being smart-arsed again. Just answer. Am I any good?
O'Toole I'm not an expert. I read only for pleasure. But I'd risk stating that I think you have a long way to go. Yet.
Armstrong You mean it's crap. Dog-shit.
O'Toole I didn't say that. It *is* interesting. Often quite fascinating. It's certainly very imaginative.

The Light around Armstrong seems to grow intense; he looks suddenly lost, far away and slightly helpless, the manuscript held, as always, close to his body

Armstrong You sound like Mr Tweedale. Mr Tweedale hated my stories and always gave me low marks. "You've got far too vivid an imagination, Armstrong—your mind's a piss-pot of obscenities—read Enid

Blyton", he said, "A. A. Milne... P. G. Wodehouse ... leave this sort of filth to the foreigners!"

O'Toole feels he is getting somewhere at last—he moves in closer, delving further, attempting to get Armstrong to open up

O'Toole Your characters, Armstrong ... do you invent them?
Armstrong (*puzzled*) I'm not sure anymore.
O'Toole Who are they, Armstrong? The mother—the daughter ... and the wife?
Armstrong Venetia.
O'Toole Venetia ... who is Venetia?
Armstrong I'm not sure. Who *is* Venetia?
O'Toole And the other man. The stranger. Who is he, Armstrong?
Armstrong It's too dangerous ... you said so yourself. Too dangerous to think about.
O'Toole Try, Armstrong. You're quite safe here. I'm with you ... try.

Silence. Distantly, softly, almost an echo, we hear "Gina Gale" singing I'll Get By. Armstrong seems to hear the music as it drifts in and out of earshot. O'Toole is quite content to wait

Armstrong He's there ... he's there now ... he's always there... (*Beat. He looks out into the dark auditorium as if trying to see something*) I imagine I live in a lighthouse ... a lighthouse far out at sea ... but, although I'd prefer it, I don't live there alone ... there's someone else, but I'm never quite sure who he is ... a friend maybe ... but whoever he is he seldom speaks...

The music dies away giving way to the sound of distant seagulls

He's no trouble really ... and yet he's always around ... waiting. And the wind blows ... and the rain lashes down ... and at night I lock and bolt the one tiny door that keeps the rest of the world out.
O'Toole (*warm, kindly, encouraging*) Go on.
Armstrong Then I climb the stone steps ... hundreds of stone steps ... to my room at the very top of the lighthouse... It's a room right under the light itself ... a small room—a warm room—cosy—with books and a fire ... and I can hear the noise of the light above me ... it creaks

Act II 51

occasionally as it turns ... turning, turning—always turning—projecting its powerful shaft of light out across the dark sea... And I'm never disturbed ... only by him ... but he's never a nuisance ... he makes no demands ... but I wish I knew what he wanted. He brings me cocoa in a mug ... cocoa and hot, buttered toast ... he lays it down then leaves the room and goes back up there for it is he who tends the light ... keeps it working—repairs it—oils it—ensures that it keeps on revolving.

O'Toole (*quietly, not wishing to break the spell*) Do you write there? Is that where you write your stories?

Armstrong What? No. Writing would spoil it all. Nor do I want to talk when I'm there. That's why I like him in a way. He doesn't want to talk either. He's like me—he's run away too.

O'Toole Run away...?

Armstrong (*as if resenting his presence*) What...?

O'Toole You said he had run away too...

Armstrong, as if to be rid of this man, rises and moves away, the manuscript still clutched to his body; he kneels C in a Light brighter now than the rest

Armstrong And in the mornings ... in the mornings when I wake and look out through my tiny window—it's fine again ... the sky is clear now ... and there's the sun—on my face. (*He holds his face up to catch the light*) And seagulls scream and race above ... they swoop and dive—swoop and dive ... and sometimes one of them will land on my windowsill and look in at me ... he looks at me—his head on one side as birds do—curious to know who I am—suspicious—cautious—one small beady eye staring in at me. I once attempted to open my window to reach out to him—but he panicked and took flight. He didn't trust me ... he was gone. But he did come back eventually ... every morning now he's there ... looking in as before ... as if checking I haven't left... (*Beat. His face changes*) But my fear ... my dread ... my awful nightmare is that one day they'll come for me. A small boat will arrive—out there. (*He points*) See ... you can almost see it. There it is—a small fishing boat—bobbing about on the sea ... with three women—or is it four? It gets nearer—maybe they won't make it ... maybe they'll drown.

A loud knocking seems to fill the auditorium

(*Listening, terrified*) Then—suddenly—there's a great knocking at the door of the lighthouse ... a loud, dreadful knocking ... bang—bang—bang!

From the darkness beyond the light come three shadowy figures. Pearl, now in a wheelchair, appears to have suffered some sort of stroke and seems unable to control the shaking of her hand—from her mouth, which is slightly distorted, there is a constant flow of saliva. The chair is being pushed by Beryl looking smart in her matching two-piece, hat, gloves and handbag—she appears more confident than before—happier, at ease. Venetia looks pale and unhappy, now dressed in Pearl's shabby mac, headscarf and carrying the same dirty canvas shopping bag on her arm

It echoes around the place ... but I'm not going down to answer... I won't let them know I'm here...
Beryl (*calling, distant*) Hallo...? Hallo, Trevor... Trevor...? It's only us, dear...
Armstrong (*calling*) Don't let them in ... please don't let them in! But it's too late ... he lets me down ... he ignores me ... now I know he's not to be trusted... I hear his footsteps on the stone stairs ... he's descending ... he's opening the door.

The knocking stops—silence. Beryl pushes her mother forward into the light which surrounds Armstrong

Beryl (*fussing*) There we are, Mum. And just look who's here. Who is it, eh? It's Trevor, isn't it? (*She wipes her mother's mouth with a clean tissue*)

O'Toole sits on the bench and lights a cigarette. Venetia remains half in shadow at a distance

It's such a long way—a whole day's excursion really—but she would insist on coming, wouldn't you, Mum? We took a coach, didn't we? Three return tickets and home by nightfall. The driver was ever so nice—chatting all the way—singing—keeping us entertained. Just the three of us on the bus—nobody else. (*Putting the finishing touches to her mother*) There we are, Mum—all tutted up now, eh...?

Act II 53

Armstrong (*not having looked at them*) What do you want? Why have you come?
Beryl And all the way the wheels of the coach seemed to be saying, "Trevor, Trevor—we're going to see our Trevor...!"
Armstrong (*loudly*) Beryl! Why are you here?
Beryl (*refusing to be intimidated*) Oh, you are funny. We've come to have a look at you. Me—and Mother—and...
Armstrong If you've brought her—if you've brought Venetia—you can tell her to frig off—I have no wish to see her.
Beryl Venetia? Here we go. Who on earth's Venetia? It's Pearl, dear. Your wife. Pearlie. Say hello, Pearl.

Venetia remains silent, in half shadow

Cyril would have come, but he's having to work late at the library. They're ever so busy—what with the cuts and the change-overs and what have you. It's often gone nine before he gets home for his supper. (*She consults her watch*) Is that clock a bit slow, Mr...?
Armstrong O'Toole. I call him O'Toole.
Beryl O'Toole—of course. Only my watch says ten past.
Armstrong All the clocks are slow in this place—it's a plot to make the days seem twice as long.
Beryl (*going over to O'Toole*) I'm sure you remember me... I'm Mrs Gunter—Beryl Gunter—Trevor's sister. We did come once before.
O'Toole (*rising, shaking her hand*) Pleased you could come again, Mrs Gunter.
Beryl We would come more often—but it's the journey. And none of us drives, you see. And what with Mother being ... well, it's not easy. (*She lowers her voice*) How is he?
Armstrong There's no need to speak in your Sunday voice, Beryl... I'm fine.
Beryl (*as if he hadn't spoken*) Will you be sending him home just yet?
O'Toole I'm afraid it's difficult to...
Beryl (*not listening*) Only ... well, it is rather awkward, Mr O'Toole. It's not that he's not wanted—far from it—but Pearl—his wife—would find it very difficult to cope. And Cyril and me—well, we do have Mother.
O'Toole You mustn't worry. We're glad to have him with us.
Beryl They have a son, you see, and, well, Pearl here thinks it might be somewhat inappropriate. (*She looks across at her brother*) His odd

behaviour and everything. (*She laughs nervously, then wanders over to the desk*) You give him pencil and paper, I see. And his little typewriter. It's a regular home-from-home for him really.
O'Toole Would you like to be left alone for a moment?
Beryl Oh no. We'd feel happier if you stayed.

O'Toole stands further off while both Beryl and Venetia stand about feeling awkward. Pearl simply shakes and dribbles, unaware of anything. Armstrong gets up knowing all eyes are upon him—he seems unsure of what blow to deliver next

Armstrong (*looking across at his mother*) She's no better, I see. Incontinent now, I suppose. Forever washing knickers, are we, Beryl?

Beryl is trying hard not to appear humiliated

"Old pissy-knicks" … is that what we call her now?
Beryl Now stop that, Trevor—please.
Armstrong (*into his mother's ear*) How was prison, dear? Nice, was it?
Beryl (*a flash of anger*) Trevor—that's enough! (*To O'Toole, embarrassed*) It's all nonsense, Mr O'Toole—he makes it all up.
Venetia Come on, Beryl—I knew this was a mistake.
Armstrong Oh, so it does speak then…
Venetia (*wanting to leave*) Beryl, please…
Armstrong How's the boy? How's little Armstrong? Misses his dad, does he, Venetia?
Venetia Please don't call me that! The boy's fine. Fine. As long as he's a million miles away from you. (*Beat*) Here, I brought you something. (*She holds out the bag*) I'd rather not have any reminders of you at home.

Armstrong turns away, refusing to accept the bag. Venetia moves down and places the bag on the bench where O'Toole sits

I'd just like you to know that I did all I could, Trevor. I tried. I tried ever so hard, but… well… I shan't be coming here again. (*Silence, then she moves to leave, and stops*) Are you coming, Beryl?

Beryl is crying softly—tears fill her eyes. She is obviously torn between what to do for the best

Act II   55

Beryl In a minute. I'll come in a minute.

Venetia gives her husband one last look, then turns and walks away into the darkness beyond the light

Silence

Armstrong (*gentler, dropping his act of bravado*) It's no use crying, Beryl. That won't solve anything.
Beryl What will you do?
Armstrong Don't worry about me. I'll be fine. I've got him, haven't I? (*He nods in O'Toole's direction*) Who knows—he might even come with me to Bangkok...

Pearl suddenly makes a sound, a noise like an abandoned animal, a cry for help almost

Beryl I think she wants to leave.
Armstrong (*turning away, his head downcast*) I'm sorry I did that to her. I'm sorry I...
Beryl It doesn't matter now. I'm sure *she* doesn't remember.

Beryl goes over to the wheelchair, wipes her mother's mouth again, then begins to push her away

Armstrong Beryl...

She stops and turns to look across at him. He picks up the discarded manuscript from where he left it on the floor

Perhaps you'd like to have this.
Beryl (*looking across at O'Toole*) But...
Armstrong It's all right. I don't want it any more. I would never have finished it anyway. Read it if you want. Then burn it.

She takes the manuscript, looks at him, then embraces him warmly and kisses his cheek, then slowly pushes her mother away into the darkness

Silence for a moment, then O'Toole rises and moves away from the bench.

He watches silently as Armstrong goes to the bench, sits, and looks down at the canvas bag, then picks it up

Who are they? Who are you? Who am I?

O'Toole doesn't answer. Out of the bag, Armstrong brings the blonde wig first, looks at it, then takes out two of the old "Gina Gale" records and looks at her photo on the sleeve

O'Toole (*quietly*) I'm sure she was real. Once.

Quietly at first, "Gina Gale" begins to sing Something To Remember You By ... *The sound grows louder*

Armstrong I did write to her, you know. I did write. (*Beat*) But she never replied...

The song grows ever louder as all the Lights begin to fade slowly to Black-out

FURNITURE AND PROPERTY LIST

ACT I

On stage: Black table. *On it:* black typewriter with paper in it, white manuscript
Black chair
Black bench
Black high stool
Standard lamp
Coat with a handkerchief in a pocket
Headscarf

Off stage: Carpet sweeper, duster, etc. (**Pearl**)
Small carpet (**O'Toole**)
Armchair, small dining table, 3 chairs, standard lamp (**All**)
Check cloth, cutlery and crockery, plates of stew (**Beryl**)
Ironing board, basket containing clothes (**Pearl**)
Knitting (**Beryl**)
Local Gazette (**Pearl**)
Old theatrical props basket on castors (**O'Toole**)
Old "Gina Gale" records, film magazines (**Venetia**)
Chair (**Pearl**)
Bench, packet of Butterkist popcorn (**Venetia**)

Personal: **O'Toole:** cigarettes, lighter
Armstrong: old-fashioned wire glasses
Venetia: nail-file
Pearl: crumpled note, handkerchief
Armstrong: schoolboy's cap
Pearl: glasses, handbag containing make-up
Beryl: tea towel
O'Toole: hand microphone
Pearl: handbag, bingo card, pen

ACT II

On stage: As before

Off stage: Wheelchair (**Pearl**)

Personal: **Armstrong:** blonde wig
Pearl: dirty canvas shopping bag, crumpled bag of boiled sweets
O'Toole: cigarettes, lighter
Armstrong: dirty towel
Beryl: bag containing home-made newsletter, handkerchief
Armstrong: pencil, knife
Beryl: handbag, tissues, wrist-watch
Venetia: dirty canvas shopping bag containing blonde wig and two old "Gina Gale" records

LIGHTING PLOT

Practical fittings required: standard lamp; mirror ball
Various interior settings

ACT I

To open: Darkness, then slowly bring up lighting on table and chair

Cue 1	**Armstrong** moves DR *Bring up lights on high stool* DR	(Page 1)
Cue 2	**O'Toole** moves L *Bring up lights on the bench* L	(Page 2)
Cue 3	**Armstrong**: "…nonsense to Venetia…" *Warmer, brighter lighting* DR	(Page 3)
Cue 4	**Armstrong** shows the upstage side of his face *Turn lighting* DR *blood red*	(Page 8)
Cue 5	**All** rearrange the set *Slowly bring up full lighting*	(Page 8)
Cue 6	**Pearl**: "The ones *he* gave me." *Fade the living-room lighting slightly; bring up lighting* DR	(Page 11)
Cue 7	**Armstrong**: "…a new frock for work … or ironing." *Bring up full living-room lighting; turn on standard lamp; bring up fire effect from proscenium*	(Page 12)
Cue 8	**Armstrong** sits in front of the glow from the "fire" *Fade lighting* DR	(Page 12)
Cue 9	Ballroom music creeps in *Slightly dip living-room lighting; bring up brighter lighting* C	(Page 14)
Cue 10	**Armstrong**: "…*he* was there, wasn't he…?" *Bring up coloured lighting down stage with mirror ball*	(Page 15)

Cue 11	**Armstrong** runs DR *Bring up lighting* DR	(Page 16)
Cue 12	**O'Toole** exits *Black-out, except for lighting* DR	(Page 16)
Cue 13	**Armstrong**: "…like most of the women in our street." *Bring up living-room lighting*	(Page 16)
Cue 14	**Armstrong** enters the scene again *Fade lighting* DR	(Page 16)
Cue 15	**Beryl**: "He was Irish too, I believe." *Fade living-room lighting*	(Page 17)
Cue 16	**Pearl** and **Beryl** exit *Bring up lighting* DR	(Page 17)
Cue 17	**Armstrong** lifts the basket lid *Bring up coloured lighting on the basket*	(Page 18)
Cue 18	**Armstrong** moves in to the living-room *Bring up living-room lighting; fade lighting* DR; *fade coloured lighting*	(Page 18)
Cue 19	**Armstrong**: "Who was O'Toole, Beryl?" *Bring up warm, pinkish pool of light*	(Page 22)
Cue 20	**O'Toole** enters *Fade living-room lighting*	(Page 22)
Cue 21	**Pearl** freezes *Bring up living-room lighting*	(Page 23)
Cue 22	**Pearl** and **O'Toole** freeze *Bring up lighting* DR	(Page 24)
Cue 23	**Armstrong**: "And it was overwhelming…!" *Cross-fade: living-room lights up fully, fade lighting* DR	(Page 25)
Cue 24	**Pearl** exits *Fade living-room lighting; bring up lighting* DR	(Page 29)
Cue 25	**Venetia** sits *Bring up soft lighting around her*	(Page 29)

Cue 26	**Armstrong** stands behind **Venetia** *Fade lighting* DR	(Page 30)
Cue 27	**Venetia**: "Oh, it's about to start." *Fade cinema lighting; start screen flicker effect*	(Page 32)
Cue 28	**Armstrong** runs R *Bring up lighting* R	(Page 32)
Cue 29	**Armstrong**'s face changes to a look of terror *Slowly fade to black-out*	(Page 33)

ACT II

To open: Darkness

Cue 30	Second verse of Gina's song is heard *Bring up spot on* **Armstrong**	(Page 34)
Cue 31	**Pearl**, **Beryl** and **O'Toole** enter *Slightly bring up lighting* DR	(Page 34)
Cue 32	**Armstrong** bows to his audience *Increase lighting* DR	(Page 34)
Cue 33	**Armstrong** runs off stage *Fade single spot*	(Page 34)
Cue 34	Sound of "Gina Gale" singing *Who's Sorry Now* *Fade lighting* DR; *bring up living-room lighting*	(Page 36)
Cue 35	Sounds of typewriter typing *Cross-fade lighting from living-room to* DL	(Page 43)
Cue 36	**Venetia** enters *Bring up lighting* DR; *bring up powerful lighting on* **Armstrong** C	(Page 44)
Cue 37	**Pearl** bounces **Armstrong** on her lap *Increase lighting on* **Armstrong**	(Page 45)
Cue 38	**O'Toole** reads the manuscript *Bring up harsh pools of white light*	(Page 45)

Cue 39	**O'Toole**: "It's certainly very imaginative." *Intensify lighting on* **Armstrong**	(Page 49)
Cue 40	**Armstrong** kneels c *Brightest lighting on* **Armstrong**	(Page 51)
Cue 41	**Armstrong**: "But she never replied…" *Slowly fade to black-out*	(Page 56)

EFFECTS PLOT

ACT I

Cue 1	To open *Music: "Gina Gale" sings*	(Page 1)
Cue 2	**Armstrong** starts work again *Fade music*	(Page 1)
Cue 3	**Armstrong** shows the upstage side of his face *Dramatic chord of music*—Phantom-of-the-Opera-ish	(Page 8)
Cue 4	**All** freeze *Music: Amen Corner singing* If Paradise Were Half as Nice	(Page 8)
Cue 5	**All** complete setting furniture and props *Cut music*	(Page 8)
Cue 6	**Pearl**: "…now you liked her." *Ballroom music*	(Page 14)
Cue 7	**O'Toole** enters *Increase music volume*	(Page 15)
Cue 8	**Venetia**: "And I'm only fifteen…!" *Cut music*	(Page 16)
Cue 9	**Armstrong**: "…invade our privacy." *Soft, distant music: orchestral version of* It's Magic	(Page 17)
Cue 10	**Armstrong**: "…change my life forever." *Increase music volume*	(Page 18)
Cue 11	**O'Toole** enters *Peak music volume*	(Page 18)
Cue 12	**Pearl** exits *After a pause, front door slams*	(Page 21)

Cue 13	**Pearl** and **O'Toole** freeze *Music: "Gina Gale" sings*	(Page 24)
Cue 14	**Beryl** grabs the record sleeve from **Armstrong** *Cut music*	(Page 25)
Cue 15	**Armstrong**: "...for a while anyway." *Music: "Gina Gale" sings*	(Page 29)
Cue 16	**Armstrong**: "...just to be near Cyril Gunter." *Fade "Gina Gale" song; bring up soft cinema music*	(Page 30)
Cue 17	**Venetia**: "Oh, it's about to start." *Fade cinema music*	(Page 32)
Cue 18	**Armstrong** and **Venetia** hold hands *Music: "Gina Gale" sings loudly, thrillingly*	(Page 32)
Cue 19	**Armstrong** runs R *Cut music*	(Page 32)

ACT II

Cue 20	To open *Music: "Gina Gale" singing an up-beat number*	(Page 34)
Cue 21	**Armstrong** slowly turns *End music; sound of rapturous applause and cheering*	(Page 34)
Cue 22	**Armstrong** runs off stage *Soft, distant music: "Gina Gale" singing* Who's Sorry Now	(Page 34)
Cue 23	**Venetia** speaks to the audience *Fade music*	(Page 35)
Cue 24	**O'Toole** walks into the darkness *Music: "Gina Gale" singing* Who's Sorry Now	(Page 36)
Cue 25	**Pearl** sits at the table *Fade music*	(Page 37)
Cue 26	**Armstrong**: "I've missed you..."	(Page 43)

Something To Remember You By

        Sound of typewriter—pounding of keyboard—ping of its bell

Cue 27   **Beryl** mimes ringing of door bell   (Page 43)
        Door bell

Cue 28   **Beryl**: "As usual."   (Page 44)
        Soft, distant music: "Gina Gale" singing Who's Sorry Now

Cue 29   **Pearl** sings   (Page 45)
        Fade music

Cue 30   **O'Toole**: "I'm with you ... try."   (Page 50)
        After a pause, distant, soft music: Kathy Kirby singing I'll Get By

Cue 31   **Armstrong**: "...but whoever he is he seldom speaks..."   (Page 50)
        Fade music; bring up sound of distant seagulls

Cue 32   **Armstrong**: "...maybe they'll drown."   (Page 51)
        Loud knocking fills the auditorium

Cue 33   **Armstrong**: "...he's opening the door."   (Page 52)
        Cut knocking

Cue 34   **O'Toole**: "Once."   (Page 56)
        Slowly fade up music: "Gina Gale" singing Something To Remember You By; *louder and louder to the end*

www.ingramcontent.com/pod-product-compliance
Ingram Content Group UK Ltd.
Pitfield, Milton Keynes, MK11 3LW, UK
UKHW021846210426
5322IPUK00022B/491